PIECES OF
WHITE SHELL

Pieces of

White Shell

A

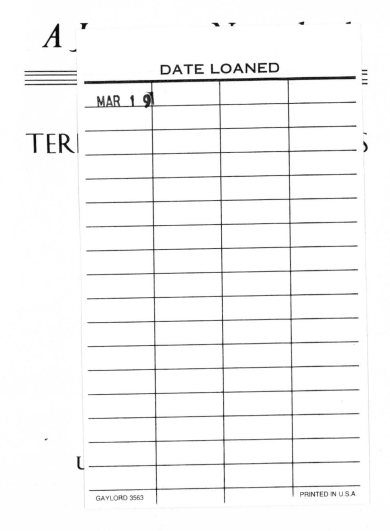

DATE LOANED

MAR 1 9			

GAYLORD 3563   PRINTED IN U.S.A.

TER

U

Portions of this book originally appeared in slightly different form in JCT: The Journal of Curriculum Theorizing, 5:4, Fall 1983, pp. 38–57.

Library of Congress Cataloging-in-Publication Data

Williams, Terry Tempest.
   Pieces of white shell.

   Bibliography: p.
   1. Navajo Indians.   I.   Title.
[E99.N3W66   1987]   978'.00498   86-24915
ISBN 0-8263-0969-0 (pbk.)

© 1983, 1984 by Terry Tempest Williams. All rights reserved.
Illustrations © 1984 by Clifford Brycelea.
University of New Mexico Press paperback edition reprinted 1987 by arrangement with Charles Scribner's Sons.

Fifth Paperbound printing, 1994

Grateful acknowledgement is made for permission to quote from the following copyrighted material:

Edward S. Ayensu, "A Worldwide Role for the Healing Powers of Plants," *Smithsonian*, November 1981, by permission of *Smithsonian*. Charlotte Johnson Frisbie, *Kinaaldá*, copyright © 1967, by permission of Wesleyan University Press. W. W. Hill, *Navaho Warfare*, Yale University Publications in Anthropology No. 5 New Haven: HRAF Press, 1970: p. 14 (reprinted from 1936 ed.). Clyde Kluckhohn, *The Navaho*, Harvard University Press, copyright © 1946 by the President and Fellows of Harvard College, reprinted by permission. Aldo Leopold, *A Sand County Almanac: With Other Essays on Conservation from Round River*, copyright © 1949, 1953, 1966, renewed 1977, 1981 by Oxford University Press, Inc., reprinted by permission. Karl W. Luckert, *Navajo Hunter Tradition*, Tucson: University of Arizona Press, copyright © 1975, used by permission. Karl W. Luckert, *Navajo Mountain and Rainbow Bridge Religion*, Museum of Northern Arizona. N. Scott Momaday, specified excerpt (p. 82), in "Native American Attitudes to the Environment," from *Seeing With a Native Eye*, ed. Walter Holden Capps, assisted by Ernst F. Tonsing. Copyright © 1976 by Walter Holden Capps. Reprinted by permission of Harper & Row, Publishers, Inc. Gladys Reichard, *Navaho Religion*, Tucson: University of Arizona Press, copyright © 1950, used by permission. Gladys Reichard, *Spider Woman*, quoted by permission of The Rio Grande Press, Inc., P O Box 33, Glorieta, N. M. 87535, from *Spider Woman*, by Gladys Reichard, title currently in print. Donald Sandner, *Navajo Symbols of Healing*, by permission of Harcourt Brace Jovanovich, Inc. Barre Toelken, specified excerpt (p. 12) in "Seeing with a Native Eye: How Many Sheep Will It Hold?," from *Seeing with a Native Eye*, ed. Walter Holden Capps, assisted by Ernst F. Tonsing. Copyright © 1976 by Walter Holden Capps. Reprinted by permission of Harper & Row, Publishers, Inc. Laurens Van der Post, *A Story Like the Wind*, by permission of William Morrow and Company, Inc. Leland C. Wyman, *Sacred Mountains of the Navajo*, Museum of Northern Arizona.

WILBRAHAM PUBLIC LIBRARY

FOR

my family

The most beautiful and most profound emotion one can experience is the sensation of the mystical. . . . It is the source of all true science.

—ALBERT EINSTEIN

CONTENTS

CONTENTS

A NOTE ON THE ARTWORK

Each illustration in *Pieces of White Shell* is made up of
two parts. The larger, more representational portion
straightforwardly illumines one aspect of the chapter; the
strip at the bottom captures the symbolic or spiritual meaning that Brycelea, as a Navajo, sees there. Each illustration
is designed to speak to the viewer as from one's heart to
another. We can all walk in beauty. In the words of the
Navajo praying:

> *In Beauty—happily—I walk*
> *With Beauty before me I walk*
> *With Beauty behind me I walk*
> *With Beauty above me I walk*
> *With Beauty all around me I walk*
> *It is finished in Beauty*
> *hozoná hăstke . . .*
> *hozoná hăstke . . .*
> *hozoná hăstke . . .*
> *hozoná hăstke.*

PROLOGUE:
A SPRIG
OF SAGE

OUT OF MY POUCH FALLS A SPRIG OF SAGE. I CAN CRUSH its leaves between my fingers and remember who I am. I belong to the Great Basin. I feel most at home in the sagebrush plains of Utah. But I haven't always been able to say this. I hated sagebrush as a child. On every family vacation, whether we drove to the California coast or to the Tetons in Wyoming, we stared hour after hour out the window at sage. Nothing seemed to move. The color seldom varied. It made me feel very ordinary.

There was another side to sage. Wood ticks loved it and so did rattlesnakes. Parents warned their children and children warned their friends. Since sagebrush covered our foothills like fur, I had encounters with both tick and snake. After a while, you just learned to put them out of your mind. Pretty soon, sagebrush didn't even exist.

Things change. Sometimes you have to disclaim your country and inhabit another before you can return to your own. Now, there is nothing as dear to me as the smell of silver sage after a rainstorm.

This book is a journey into one culture, Navajo, and back out again to my own, Mormon. I am reminded by a Shoshone friend that I come to the Navajo as a migrating bird, lighting for only brief periods of time. This is true. But it is also true that the lessons I learn come from similar places. No one culture has dominion over birdsong. We all share the same sky.

The path I travel is the path where my ancestors' bones lie: in the four corners of Utah, Colorado, New Mexico, and Arizona. Navajoland stretches thousands of miles across this region, encompassing over sixteen million acres in all. We are neighbors.

We are both relative newcomers to the land. Navajo migration patterns appear from the late 1300s to the 1500s, with Athabaskan ancestors coming into the American Southwest from an original homeland in western Canada and Alaska. My people's genesis is in the early 1800s, with pilgrimages from New York to Nauvoo, to Utah.

As a result of our histories, we both have a strong sense of locale. The Navajo's world emerged with each living thing bearing record of the next: All were relatives, the land their Mother. Brigham Young in 1847 stood on the threshold of the Salt Lake Valley and spoke four words: "This is the place."

There are problems. Navajos find themselves caught between modernization and tradition. So do Mormons. People question us. There are tensions. Self-preservation fosters naivete and shrewdness.

We are a spiritual people, Mormon and Navajo. We believe in a power that moves us, directs us, cares for us. We are taught to listen. The Navajo have their sacred mountains and we have our sacred groves and temples. Family ties are extended and strong. These are not exclusive characteristics. I merely highlight similarities of background.

But there are major differences, primarily in the stories we tell and the way in which we walk upon the earth. It is here that I am most aware of leaving my own culture and entering another. I take off my shoes and walk barefoot. There are risks, I know. My feet have been cut many times, but I am learning to pay attention.

Of the Navajo Way, Gladys Reichard says in *Navaho Religion*, "It must be considered as a design in harmony, a striving for rapport between man and every phase of nature, the earth and the waters under the earth, the sky and the land beyond the sky, and, of course, the earth and everything on and in it."

Navajo stories have been my guides across the desert. I have trusted them because I could find no others. They are rooted in native soil. To these people they are sacred. Truth. To me, they are beacons in a nation suspicious of nature.

A story grows from the inside out and the inside of Navajoland is something I know little of. But I do know myself and if I begin traveling with an awareness of my own ignorance, trusting my instincts, I can look for my own stories embedded in the landscapes I travel through.

A story allows us to envision the possibility of things. It

draws on the powers of memory and imagination. It awakens us to our surroundings. I can follow an owl into a cottonwood grove or listen for Kokopeli's flute. I can sit in the
crepuscular hours of a day or imagine a snake uncoiling
from a basket. It is here, by our own participation in nature,
that we pick up clues to an awareness of what a story is.
Story making comes out of our life experiences. And there
are many, many layers we can penetrate.

Storytelling is the oldest form of education. It is the
power of image making. Among Native Americans the
oral tradition of a tribe is its most important vehicle for
teaching and passing on sacred knowledge and practices of
the people. Luther Standing Bear, a Lakota, recalls:

> Lakota children, like all others, asked questions and
> were answered to the best ability of our elders. We
> wondered, as do all young, inquisitive minds, about
> the stars, moon, sky, rainbows, darkness, and all
> other phenomena of nature. I can recall lying on the
> earth and wondering what it was all about. The
> stars were a beautiful mystery and so was the place
> where the eagle went when he soared out of sight.
> Many of these questions were answered in story
> form by the older people. How we got our pipestone,
> where corn came from, and why lightning flashed
> in the sky were all answered in stories.

Maria Chona, a Papago woman, explains how a child
learned among her people:

> My father went on talking to me in a very low voice.
> This is how our people always talk to their children,
> so low and quiet, the child thinks he is dreaming.
> But he never forgets.

And then I asked Harold Drake of Navajo Mountain why stories are told.

"I will tell you this: They are for the children generation after generation."

I am not suggesting we emulate Native Peoples—in this case, the Navajo. We can't. We are not Navajo. Besides, their traditional stories don't work for us. It's like drinking another man's medicine. Their stories hold meaning for us only as examples. They can teach us what is possible. We must create and find our own stories, our own myths, with symbols that will bind us to the world as we see it today. In so doing, we will better know how to live our lives in the midst of change.

We have a tradition in our family that centers around the Christmas tree. It began with the birth of the first grandchild.

In 1955, my grandmother placed an angel with gossamer wings on top of a tiny tree. Other angels were hung on lower branches, along with a menagerie of beaded animals and a red bird made of ash. She hung the little bird on an outside limb to give it the appearance of flight. These were the "original" ornaments.

As the family grew, the tree grew. In the next few years, other grandchildren were born—seven boys and a girl. To accompany the angels and animals, my grandmother introduced clowns, elves, harlequins, and varieties of Santa Claus. The tree slowly became animated, so much so that the children would often ask each other if they had ever seen it move.

Each year new ornaments were added—picked for a particular child or event. Crocheted pandas were placed on the tree to symbolize endangered species, an alligator was sent from Florida by a grandchild who was living there, and gold bells hung on the branches to celebrate our grandparents' fiftieth wedding anniversary. Wooden stars, satin moons, saw-whet owls, skiers, a llama from Bolivia, and angels from every country—all held special significance. Other ornaments represented the darker side of life. As my grandmother would explain, there must always be two poles. And so every year we would look for the new "voodoo" as well as the "saint."

The Sunday following Thanksgiving weekend, that magical day, is "the day the tree goes up." As each ornament is taken out of its box and unwrapped it is like seeing an old friend. The women sit on the couches and talk, fixing broken treasures and supplying hooks for objects that need them. The men stretch out on the floor and sleep, occasionally opening their eyes to see how things are progressing while we children hang our personal histories on the tree.

After the last angel is placed, the boys stand back and throw ribbon-birds (blue, pink, and purple; green, orange, and yellow) onto the tree—the reckless, spontaneous finish.

Today the tree is an internal tree as well, our family tree. It continues to grow as we grow. My grandparents are in their seventies now. Last year, I asked my grandmother if she would write the saga of the tree, what story each ornament told. "We could do it together," I said. She smiled and said, "Yes, let's do." But I knew that behind her twinkling eyes she had other thoughts.

In 1982 the tree went up just as it had done for almost thirty years. The candles were lit. The fire was burning and

Leontyne Price sang "Ave Maria." As we nestled into our chairs, my grandmother began to tell her story.

"You see, this tree is alive. . . ."

And she went into the layers of memories. I could feel the heat of the fire massaging my back. I marveled at her animation.

While my grandmother spoke of blue-eyed zebras and quail, I thought I heard the fluttering of wings. I didn't pay much attention until I heard them for the second time. I interrupted to ask if anyone else had heard the sound. Everyone just laughed, saying, "You always hear wings." My grandmother went on. "So you see why we think this tree is alive—"

Just then, a small bird flew down from the chimney, through the flames of the fire, and onto a branch of the tree. It was a weaver finch. No one could speak. A living ornament. He stood on the bough as though it were his favorite perch in the forest. He then circled the tree three times, flew over to the corner of the living room, hit the copper chimes, and landed back underneath the tree with all the animals.

By this time, we had acknowledged the bird's presence and were concerned about getting him back outside. Instinctively, I knelt under the tree with cupped hands and coaxed the bird into them. My fingers wrapped around him and I could feel the rapid heartbeat moving his feathers. There were several quick chirps but no singed wings. I forget who opened the door. The next thing I remember is crouching barefoot in the snow with the finch underneath a yew bush. I waited for some time, softly speaking to the little bird. And then he flew. The night was crystalline. As I walked back into the warm house, my grandmother put her arms around me as my grandfather quietly said, "The story's been written."

I offer you a sampling of the Navajo voice, of my voice, and the voice of the land that moves us. We are told a story and then we tell our own. Each of us harbors a homeland. The stories that are rooted there push themselves up like native grasses and crack the sidewalks.

A few years ago, my cousin Lynne Ann moved to Boston. She could hardly wait to leave Utah and plunge into city life. I told her, "One day you will miss these foothills." We laughed. That Christmas I received a card from her. It read: "Please send me some sage—"

I

CURATOR

I AM A COLLECTOR. ON MY DESK SITS A SMALL LEATHER pouch, weatherbeaten, full of mementos of the desert. I have carried it with me everywhere in Navajoland. It is my link with the Diné, as they call themselves. I am shy. The people are shy. The objects inside give us courage to speak.

I shake the objects out of their pouch and spread them across my desk. What stories they tell: a sprig of sage; rocks, sand, and seeds; turquoise, obsidian, coral; pieces of white shell; yucca; a bouquet of feathers bound by yarn; coyote fur; a bone from Black Mountain; deerskin; wool; a potshard and some corn pollen. Wait—something is missing. I shake the pouch four more times and from the bottom of the bag rolls out the Storyteller, a clay figurine from Jemez.

Nothing unusual. Just the sort of paraphernalia you would expect to find on a curator's desk at the Utah Museum of Natural History.

I am new here. When interviewed for this job, I was asked if there were any problems I could foresee.

"Just one," I said. "Everything in this museum is dead, past tense." I saw a look of astonishment come over the director's face. ". . . beautifully dead and remarkably old," I tried to rephrase, but I could see there would be no retraction.

I also made the mistake of asking my superior if the museum had done any research on the long-term effects of mothball inhalation. This was a concern of mine as I knew I would be spending considerable time with the bird skins. He assured me there was nothing to worry about, since they were now using a new insect deterrent called Edolan U, which had previously been used in the dry cleaning business. It is guaranteed to be safe for humans and most effective in feather preservation. My mind was eased. I was hired in spite of my candor.

As the director took me around the museum, I sensed good humor in the staff. Jay, the artist responsible for exhibits, moonlights on the side by painting fiberglass fish. As I admired his mounts, I commented on how iridescent the belly scales were, very lifelike.

"Thank you," he said. "I'm quite pleased with this discovery of mine. It's called purple pearl. You can buy it in bulk at Zim's Create-A-Craft."

Evidently a neighbor who paints plastic grapes had introduced him to this special glaze and that has made all the difference in his fish.

I could not be as enthusiastic about the freeze-dried reptiles. Freeze drying is a new technique used by museums across the country to preserve reptile specimens in natural-looking poses. People could never mistake a freeze-dried rattlesnake in a defensive coil for a living one about to strike. Or could they? We are not accustomed to looking into a snake's eyes, or those of any other animal for that matter. Too threatening.

As my museum tour continued, Don Hague, the director, was full of stories. He explained the misunderstanding that sometimes exists between the public and museums. About six years ago, for example, the University of Utah discovered that Brigham Young University, a private institution to the south, had a male Anasazi corpse which the museum wished to borrow. A representative from the museum was sent down to retrieve the mummy. Don went. He picked up the mummy right on schedule and carefully placed him in the back of his Ford station wagon. He placed the sun-parched remains in a translucent body bag. Very routine. The aboriginal figure measured almost six feet in length, making it a tight fit to accommodate both head and feet. No worry, Salt Lake City was only forty miles away. The mission seemed accomplished.

While driving home from Provo, Don decided to make a quick stop at the Lehi Drive-In. They have an unusually good reputation for chicken-on-a-bun. When he returned to his car, there stood half the population of Lehi gazing in the windows. Suspicion of homicide hung in the air. Luckily, Don could defend himself by showing the official transfer papers, legitimizing the mummy's release from

B.Y.U., but that did little to erase the puzzled scowls of the townspeople.

Across the courtyard, past Cottam's Gulch, we entered Collections. It was here I saw the seriousness of museums. We were met by a tall, thoughtful woman named Ann, who is curator of Collections. We had interrupted her work under the microscope.

"It's not my work," she said affectionately. "It's my love affair."

I looked into the lens and saw filaments of light twisted around each other.

"Yucca," she said.

With gloved hands, she carefully removed the basket fragment from underneath the scope and placed it in its storage case. Don left. I stayed and followed her into the next room.

"This is where we keep the artifacts," she said.

We closed the door. I stood before the corridors of objects and felt disoriented. In these drawers were *atlatyls, manos, metates,* digging sticks, pots, bowls, baskets, awls, muskrat nests, capes of rabbit skin, scrapers, projectile points, feathered slippers, saddles, Navajo blankets, and bones—their identities confused in a context not their own. If it is possible to hear the voice of an artifact, I heard many songs.

I watched Ann. She said nothing. A silver bracelet held her wrist.

Stories. Everyone, everything carries a story. A story brings life and definition to the mundane. It animates and enthralls.

Just yesterday, I was told that the Bighorn sheep downstairs was transplanted from the Canadian Rockies to Utah's Oquirrh Range. On one occasion, he wandered down to the west desert and mixed with a flock of domestic sheep. For days he was trying to mount every available ewe. Finally, a herder shot him.

"He was causing a lot of trouble," the old man said. And so here he stands. I look at that ram differently now.

My mind wanders. It is a typical Salt Lake summer and the building has no air-conditioning. I am sweating and uncomfortable. Irony. I am reminded of days when the desert heat healed me, forcing me to walk barefoot and exposed. As I come back to these desert treasures scattered across my desk, I become homesick for a place that is not my home. But I have relatives there. I lean back into my chair, close the door, and dream of turquoise skies until I can feel warm breezes carrying the scent of sage.

2

ROCKS, SAND, AND SEEDS

BE CAREFUL OF YOUR FIRST IMPRESSIONS OF THIS COUNTRY. It disarms you. It can be hostile. I have an aunt who lives in Nephi, Utah. Her name is Martha Cazier Egar. At ninety, she still remembers with fondness her sister Adrienne's words as she stepped off the bus from new York: "Mattie, this is the most godforsaken place I've ever seen! No wonder Mother writes you so often."

"What did you say to her?" I asked.

"I said, 'Adrienne, give the country a chance.'"

Aunt Mattie and Uncle Jim lived in Shiprock, New Mexico, among the Navajo in the 1930s. Jim worked for the Soil Conservation Service, a division of the Department of Agriculture. They took Adrienne by the hand, let her swim in rivers, and courted her with sunsets. They had picnics on mesa tops and crushed sage in stews. Mattie even had her sister helping in the garden, nurturing gourds.

Mattie always planted gourds for the Indians. She had the fun of watching them grow, then in the fall after the harvest would leave them in a pile in front of her house. The people always knew they were for them. They used them in ceremonies.

"When Adrienne left us, she cried," Aunt Mattie said. "She told us we lived in a very special place, and to tell the other kin they need at least three days to get used to it!"

Give the country a chance—that's what Aunt Mattie says. You will find yourself in unfamiliar territory at first, where the vastness is disquieting, the starkness leaves you empty. You will walk among rocks that tell time differently. Your skin will burn and your hair will lighten. You will find a waterhole and kneel with cupped hands. The reflection you see will not be of the person you once were. Neither is the land.

I first came to Navajoland as a teacher. I was curious to see the desert from the children's perspective. In Ramah, New Mexico, I stood before a classroom of seven-year-olds. I told them I came from the city where earth is covered with tar and cement, where skyscrapers stand as canyon walls. Some laughed. Others looked puzzled.

"I don't really know what lies in the desert—what lives and breathes. Take me on an imaginary walk. Show me what you see. Let's make a list."

The children took their time. I fidgeted with the chalk.

Several seconds passed. Maybe even a minute or two. No response. I cleared my throat. The silence was uncomfortable, almost unbearable, until it became a metaphor of how one approaches the land: with silence, with patience, and with time. The children know.

I could feel their thoughts stirring the room. But the room was closed to me. The children were doubled up in secrets. I was a goose in a flock of teals. Many giggled. Others stared down at their feet.

"Lizards!" one boy blurted. "I see lizards."

He broke the classroom open. What followed reminded me of an August night in Wyoming when I was lying on my back waiting for the Perseus Shower. A meteor flashed across the sky, then another, and another. And suddenly there was an explosion of light, with twenty or thirty shooting stars every minute. So it was with the children. They began sharing their desert discoveries at such a pace I couldn't write them on the chalkboard fast enough:

ROCKS
SAND
SEEDS
RATTLESNAKE
HORNED TOAD
BONES
YUCCA
FEATHERS
TREASURES
WORMS
BEES
STINK BUGS
HORSES
SHEEP
GOATS

FOSSILS
PINYONS
LIONS
DEER
BEAR
BROKEN POTTERY
BATS
ARROWHEADS
CHUCKWAGON
OLD CLOTHES
WEEDS
GRAVEYARDS
CLOUDS
STARS
MUD
SHADE HOUSE
ROADRUNNER
FLOWERS
RAIN
LAKE
ANTS
FLIES
INSECTS
TURTLES
WINDMILLS
PORCUPINES
TRACKS
SKINWALKERS
COYOTE
OWLS
RAVEN
CROW
SKULLS
PLANTS
NAVAJO TEA
MESAS

SKY
HOGAN
CORN
MICE
DEAD RATS
PEOPLE
TREES
EAGLES
CLIFFS
VULTURES
BIRDS
MOTHS
TARANTULAS
RUINS
SNAKES
FOX
BOTTLES
SWALLOWS
WOLFMAN JACK
BUTTERFLIES
JAWS
OLD GUNS
FRY BREAD
TRAILS
BULLETS
BONES
MORE BONES
SUN
MOON
SAGE

And footprints. The children's footprints.

Geologically speaking, Navajoland lies within the Colorado Plateau. The Colorado Plateau is characterized by horizontal, sedimentary formations, deeply incised drainage systems, aridity, and sparse vegetation. It is a physiographic province bordered by the Great Basin to the west and the Rocky Mountains to the north and east.

During the Paleozoic era, about 600 million years ago, this land was periodically covered by shallow seas. The shoreline migrated west, exposing broad tracts of ancient seabeds. These earliest rocks are exposed only in the deepest canyons.

During the Mesozoic era, 225 million to 70 million years ago, the scene changed dramatically. The seas retreated again and an interior basin was created due to the rise of the Mesocordilleran High on one side and the ancestral Rocky Mountains on the other. At this time, nonmarine deposits were laid by wind and water. Evidence of this process can be found in Navajo sandstone which once stood as dunes, Kayenta and Moenave formations which were once stream deposits, and the Chinle formation which speaks of both lake and stream deposits with traces of volcanic ash. These formations were laid in the Triassic period.

During the late Jurassic, a brief incursion from the north took place as a narrow seaway flowed through. The deposits from the sea produced the Carmel and Twin Creeks formations. Finally, seas flooded the Colorado Plateau once again, ending the Cretaceous period of the Mesozoic era. Imagine coal forming lagoons and bayous along the shoreline—the transformation today being the Kaiparowitz Plateau and mancos shale.

In the Cenozoic era, the seas were expelled as North America was uplifted. Superimposed on this continental uplift were numerous local areas of more dramatic crustal activity: areas such as the Uinta Mountains, the San

Rafael Swell, the Uncompahgre, the Kaibab Plateau, and the Monument Upwarp. It is referred to by geologists as the "Laramide Orogeny," which took place sometime between 60 to 40 million years ago. This was the beginning of the modern topography of the Colorado Plateau as we know it.

Also during this time, lakes began to develop in the lowlands between uplifts. Watersheds were created. The Claron formation of Bryce Canyon and the Green River formation are testimonials to these past lakebeds.

As surface upheavals continued, an intense downcutting of streams and an integration of drainages took place. This action is largely responsible for the development of the spectacular canyons associated with the Southwest. The law of uniformitarianism tells us that what happened then is still happening today. What is left of the Colorado River continues to cut.

Volcanic rocks spewn across the Colorado Plateau are reminiscent of eruptions during late Cenozoic time. Shallow intrusions of magma slowly worked their way to the surface, appearing as blisters rather than explosions due to the thickness of the earth's crust. The Henry, La Sal, and Abajo mountains are all examples of this process. They have been raised by an igneous fist. Remnants of true volcanic eruptions are Agatha Peak, the Hopi diatremes, and Shiprock. Standing as black spires, they are the throats of volcanoes.

These rocks tell other stories as well. Even if one were not sensitive to the mythical happenings here, the imagination would have to be piqued.

There were two sons born to Sun and Changing Woman: Monster Slayer and Child-of-the-waters.

They were twins . . . although they overcame the monsters one by one, it was impossible to obliterate their carcasses. Consequently, the Navajo country is still littered with unburied remnants of their bodies. Big Monster, for example, is thought to have lived near Mt. Taylor. After killing him, The Twins cut off his head and threw it far to the east, where it now stands as Cabezon Peak (Spanish Head). The blood of Big Monster flowed in a great stream down the valley until stopped by the flint club of Monster Slayer. It coagulated and may now be seen as the lava formation in the vicinity of McCarty's Wash. Another time The Twins raised a storm to kill other monsters whose heads may still be seen as volcanic peaks around the base of Mt. Taylor.

Similarly, Shiprock, Tsé Bit'a'i or The-rock-with-wings, is viewed as once being the home of the *Tse'na'hale*, a pair of creatures resembling gigantic eagles. They lived on Tsé Bit'a'i and caught and devoured people. The pair were fierce and strong, and it was feared they would soon destroy everyone.

One day, Monster Slayer asked his Grandmother, "Mother, Grandmother, tell me where do the *Tse'na'hale* dwell?"

"They dwell at Tsé Bit'a'i," she answered. "But do not venture near them. They are ferocious beasts."

The next morning Monster Slayer sneaked away, taking with him an intestine filled with blood from a previously slain monster. He traveled over the mountains until he came to the place where two great snakes lay. He walked along the backs of the snakes, alternating from one to the next. He moved with tremendous speed. Finally, he reached the plains that gave birth to Tsé Bit'a'i. There he saw the magnificent black rock that looks like a bird. He approached the rock boldly.

Suddenly, Monster Slayer heard a rushing sound overhead, much like that of a deadly whirlwind. Looking up, he saw the male *Tse'na'hale*. The warrior barely had time to throw himself on the ground before the *Tse'na'hale* swooped over him. Three times Monster Slayer escaped. But on the fourth time, coming from the north, the monster seized him in his talons and flew off to Tsé Bit'a'i.

The *Tse'na'hale* circled higher and higher with Monster Slayer until he was dropped onto the ledge where they reared their young. This was the way victims were customarily killed. Monster Slayer, however, saved himself by drawing out the life-feather that had been given to him by Spider Woman. He floated to safety at the mercy of the breezes.

When Monster Slayer landed he cut open his bag of blood and let it flow over the rocks so the *Tse'na'hale* would think he had been killed. But trouble was not over for the warrior as he soon discovered two young *Tse'na'-hale*. They cried up to their father, "This thing is not dead; it says 'Shh!' at us."

"That is only air escaping from the body," said the father. "Never mind and eat it." Then he flew away in search of other prey.

When the old bird was gone, Monster Slayer asked the young ones when their parents would be back.

"They will return after the he-rain and the she-rain. Look for them on these cliffs," they replied.

Monster Slayer could see the crags to the north and south. He positioned himself behind a rock and waited. Before long it began to rain; the thunder rolled and lightning flashed. The male *Tse'na'hale* returned and Monster

Slayer hurled his lightning arrow at the monster. *Tse'na'hale* tumbled to the foot of Winged Rock.

After a while it began to rain again, but this time there was no thunder and no lightning. Just as the young birds had said, the female *Tse'na'hale* landed on the rocky crags to the left. Monster Slayer threw another lightning arrow and sent her body down to join her mate's. The people were saved. The long lava dike to the southwest of Shiprock is said to be the blood of these Cliff Monsters.

I cannot pick up a piece of lava without squirming a bit, knowing it once flowed through the veins of Big Monster. There is still blood on the reservation today. You can wipe it up with a towel in the streets of border towns.

3

TURQUOISE,
OBSIDIAN,
AND
CORAL

IF YOU SIT ON THE CANYON'S EDGE, LOOKING DOWN, YOU
watch the end of a day. This is the place where tall shadows dwell. They stretch across the land, their heads tower-
ing over me. When they arrived, I am not certain. How
they move about in such stillness, only Sun could betray
their secret.

Colors winnow out from the fading light. What was grey
becomes aquamarine. A pale aster is now amethyst. Row
after row of sleeping women float above heatwaves. These
are not obscure mountain ranges. They are desert profiles.

An evening primrose blooms and then another. I hold

out my hands and make bird shadows on the sandstone. I hear the whistling of dove flight and the song of canyon wren. Violet-green swallows, white-throated swifts, and nighthawks wing their way through rock mazes and circle first stars. I watch vultures soar and see clay-colored mammals traverse the flats. My feet are startled by the black-and-white flickerings of King Snake. I look across —only a few seconds of sunset remain.

Is that Bobcat that skirts my vision? I cannot be sure. The warm desert winds blow through me. Insects also pass. They are metallic chimes. Who knows about this desert? I may be here for days. Perhaps I shall be an arch tomorrow.

Out of my pouch spills turquoise, obsidian, and coral. They are stones I have picked up in my travels. I feel their weight against my palm. They remind me of things I have seen. Now, as I look at them together—blue, black, and red—they become bluebird, raven, and red tail, or perhaps day sky, night sky, and dawn. Only the Navajo weaver inspired by Spider Woman can unleash these colors to fly across her loom.

Color is of primary importance throughout Navajo life. The Diné believe they have migrated upward through four worlds, thought of as superimposed hemispheres. Each is supported by pillars made of precious stones: four of whiteshell to the east, four of turquoise to the south, four of abalone to the west, and four of redstone to the north. These sky pillars, called Those-who-stand-under-the-sky, are regarded as deities. The reed of emergence, in a sacred, unexplainable way, made it possible for The People to move from one world into the next.

The space between the hemispheres is filled with stars.

How did they get there? Sacred Beings. Black God, First Man, and First Woman laid the stars on a blanket on the ground. Black God placed the Sq'tsoh (North Star). First Man placed the Náhookqs (Big Dipper), while First Woman put the Nákoqkos (Little Dipper) into the sky. After First Man and First Woman had named the main constellations and placed them in the sky, they instructed the stars to guard the sky and man forever.

Before First Man was finished meticulously placing each star in its predestined spot, Coyote came along and asked what they were doing. Intrigued, Coyote picked up a star and hung it in the south, saying, "This is my Sq'Doo Nídízídí (Morning Star)." And then he went about his business.

Later on, Coyote returned. Seeing how slowly the naming and placement of the stars were progressing, he took a corner of the blanket and flipped the remaining stars into the sky, creating the Milky Way. First Man scolded Coyote for his impulsive act, but Coyote felt he had done a fine deed.

Navajo mythology is bathed in stardust. Crosses depicting stars occur not only on ceremonial paraphernalia, but in sacred sand paintings as well. Anyone who gazes upon an open sky in the Southwest finds the constellations imprinted on his eyelids for nights to come.

It is known among the Navajo that each constellation represents a law which the people must obey. When the Diné stop obeying the laws which are written in the sky, the Navajo tribe will come to an end.

Celestial wisdom finds its roots in story:

> . . . First Woman, after all the stars were placed in the sky, said, "Now all the laws our people will need

are printed in the sky where everyone can see
them. . . . The commands written in the stars must
be obeyed forever."

I was walking down a dirt road in Chinle, Arizona. It
was well after dusk. An old man approached. We stopped
and talked. We listened to each other celebrate the night,
as the Big Dipper rested on the western horizon.

"You know the Milky Way is the path of souls . . ." he
said.

A crescent moon hung over a hogan and the stars
seemed especially bright. I watched a satellite travel across
the sky. Skylab had just fallen to earth somewhere in
Australia. I thought about what the old man had just said
so casually. I looked up to the sky once again. The
Pleiades were as they had always been.

Sandoval, the Navajo medicine man, made a simple
statement about order in the Navajo Universe: "There was
a plan from the stars down. . . ." Following the placement
of stars came the placement of Sun and Moon.

First Man and First Woman wanted a stronger light to
awaken them in the morning and a light to guide them
during the night. They spread six buckskins on the
ground. On them they placed a perfect piece of turquoise.
It was large and round. They marked the great turquoise
with a mouth, nose, and eyes. Then they streaked the face
with yellow and placed six more buckskins on top of it.
This became Jóhónaa'ei, or Sun.

Next they placed a perfect piece of white shell on a
buckskin. This was to become Tl'éhonaa'éí, or Moon.
After great difficulty, Sun and Moon were moved and

placed in the sky. The Sun Carrier and Moon Carrier declared that each day as they journeyed from east to west, someone would die. This would be the price they exacted for carrying the Sun and the Moon.

To become intimate with the sky, Sun, and Moon, we climb mountains. And to the Navajo, all of the *nahasdzáán bikáá' niilyáii*, or Things-that-were-put-on-the-surface-of-the-earth, hold great significance.

> Mountains represent parts of the earth's body—heart, skull, breast, and internal organs—and, like the body of an earth person, they have the power of motion, given them by the Winds.

The Navajo identify four sacred mountains which border the reservation today. They all have mythical origins.

In the Fourth World, First Man and First Woman forced the four main sacred mountains from the soil that First Man had gathered from the mountains in the Third World. Each mountain has corresponding colors, precious stones, and animals dependent upon the direction it faces.

Floyd Laughter, a member of the Red-streak-in-water clan, shares his knowledge of such things:

> Each of these mountains has a story, prayer, song, and ceremony associated with it. And all are interconnected including the sacred songs. And within that sacred land we were born, and continue to be born. And within this sacred land we will reach old age. This was laid down and decreed for us from the beginning. But nowadays, on tops of many of these mountains, towers have been built. But I still use some of them. I still give my prayers and offerings.
> . . . these mountains have been set up as our, our

Constitution. Yes, it is like the very same thing which the white people call their Constitution. For us these four mountains were set up and sanctified for that same purpose.

These mountains include Blanca Peak, or Sis Naajiní, located on the eastern border of Navajoland. First Man and First Woman fastened Sis Naajiní to the earth with a bolt of white lightning.

They covered the mountain with a blanket of daylight, and they decorated it with white shells, white lightning, black clouds, and male rain. They placed the white shell basket on the summit; and in this basket two eggs of the pigeons. They said that the pigeons were to be the mountain's feather. And they sent Bear to guard the doorway of White Bead Boy in the east.

Mt. Taylor, Tso dził, is located in the south. Here, it is said, First Man and First Woman fastened the mountain to earth with a stone knife.

They covered this mountain of the south with a blue cloud blanket; and they decorated it with turquoise, white corn, dark mists, and female rain. They placed a turquoise basket on the highest peak, and in it they put two eggs of the Bluebird. Bluebirds are Tzo dził's feathers. They sent Big Snake to guard the doorway of Turquoise Boy in the south.

The Mountain guarding the west is San Francisco Peak, Dook'o'oosłiid, where it was fastened to earth with a sunbeam.

First Man and First Woman covered the mountain of the west with a yellow cloud. They adorned it with haliotis shell, yellow corn, black clouds, and the male rain, and they called many animals to dwell upon it. They placed the abalone shell basket on the summit, and in it they placed the two eggs of yellow warbler. These birds were to become its feathers. Black Wind was told to go to the west and guard the doorway of Abalone Shell Boy.

Hesperus Peak, Dibéntsàá, is the sacred mountain to the north. It was fastened by First Man and First Woman to earth by a rainbow.

Over it they spread a blanket of darkness. They decorated it with obsidian, black vapors, and different plants and animals. The basket they placed on its highest peak was of obsidian, and in it they put two eggs of blackbird. The blackbirds are the mountain's feathers. Lightning was sent to guard Jet Boy's doorway in the north.

North, south, west, and east; black, blue, yellow, and white. The spiritual nature assigned to these peaks rouses me to look again at our own mountains. What I think is intimacy may not be intimacy at all.

There have been mornings in Utah when I appreciated the Wasatch Range. Many when I have not. The mountains are always there. It is I who fade in and out of the valley.

One morning in February I was on my way to teach for the museum. A group of third-graders was waiting. I picked up a film, walked out the door, and was struck by a prism of light suspended above Mt. Olympus from an unexpected opening. It was a dilation of rainclouds. I continued walking toward my car. Once again, I thought I heard the faint whirring of wings. It became stronger and stronger until suddenly, from the south, came a bird with lightning speed. I looked up and recognized the slate-blue helmet of a peregrine falcon, the clear white feathers in the creases of his wings.

Before I realized what had happened the falcon was gone, the rainbow was gone, and I was left standing in Salt Lake City with a class to teach in twenty minutes. I had been wondering what I could say to the children.

4

PIECES
OF
WHITE
SHELL

PIECES OF WHITE SHELL. I WOULD NEVER THINK OF ASSOCI-
ating these gifts from the ocean with the desert. But then, I
am not Navajo. My knowledge of earth is literal, with dis-
tinct categories and fixed points. I have always been told
you find seashells on the beach, pinecones in the forest,
and bleached bones on the desert. I have believed in pre-
dictabilities, but should I wander awhile? Remove myself
from asphalt paths. Take off my shoes. Unbraid my hair.
Forget biological rules and constraints. Then could I see
Pacific waves roll in, carrying pinecones from the sea? Or
dream of fragile, fertile possibilities—of seashells dangling

from the boughs of lodgepole pines? Perhaps even expect to see bare, bleached bones resume their stance in life? Pieces of white shell in the desert? White shell, the currency between cultures.

I have a friend in Shiprock whose name is Martina Merriboy. How we became acquainted is not as important as what we shared. We found our connection in pieces of white shell.

I had in my pouch a clam shell from Third Beach on the Olympic Peninsula. I wanted Martina to have it. A gift. Mine, now hers. As she held it in her hands, I sensed an intimacy.

"This is White Shell," she said. "My grandmother hung pieces across the top of my cradleboard."

"Why?" I asked hesitantly, not wanting to intrude on private thoughts.

"Shináli, my grandmother, did not want me to forget. . . ."

"Forget what?" I inquired.

And she began to tell a story:

Not so very long ago, First Man and First Woman noticed that a large, purple raincloud had been hovering for four consecutive days over Chi'ool'i'i', Governador Knob, the central sacred mountain. Finally, the clouds lifted, and they could see the mountain was covered with rain, an indication that supernatural events were taking place. Carrying a song in his mind, First Man decided to approach the mountain. From the bottom, he heard a baby cry; and he sang his way to the summit. There he discovered a beautiful baby girl in a cradle made of sky messengers; two short rainbows lay longitudinally under the baby, supporting her back, with red sunrays running crosswise over her chest and feet. A curved rainbow arched over her face, with pieces of white shell and turquoise dangling below. Wrapped in a purple raincloud, the infant was covered with dark blue, yellow, and white clouds, held in tightly by side lacings of zigzag lightning with a sunbeam laced through them.

First Man did not know what to do with the baby, so he took her home to First Woman, who with the aid and wisdom of Talking God raised her.

The eyes of this newly found babe were black as obsidian, and there were no blemishes or impurities anywhere on her body. First Man, Woman, and Talking-god agreed she should be fed the foods of Gods: moistened pollen with game broth and the dew of beautiful wildflowers. So nourished, she grew remarkably fast, incredibly wise, and with miraculous speed.

"This is the birth of Estsánatlehi, or Changing Woman," Martina said. "Some people say she was made from a piece of turquoise and has a younger sister, Yolkai Estan, made from white shell. One is related to earth, and one is related to water. I believe they are the same."

Changing Woman. Martina and I have gone our separate ways, but the images she created for me stand bright and illuminated, much like the full moon over Tsé Bit'a'i, Shiprock.

The miraculous birth of Changing Woman enhances her mystique. In a sense, her birth bridges the gap between The People and The Gods. Changing Woman is benevolent. She is the constant bearer of verdant gifts.

The next episode in the life of Changing Woman is her

impregnation by Sun. Mythology suggests that light and water are essential for conception. Sun stands for heat as well as light; water symbolizes semen. This is a recurring motif in origin myths. When Changing Woman first became mature she had not learned about sexual intercourse, but in trying to satisfy her desires let the sun shine into her vagina; at noon when Sun stopped to feed his horse, she went to a spring and let water drip into her.

Two similar accounts record the impregnation of Changing Woman, the last version being in compliance with the simultaneous birth of Whiteshell Woman:

> Going to gather seeds, she met the white creature on a white horse with white trappings who turned out to be Sun. He instructed her to meet him in an especially prepared brush shelter. First Man built this for her and Sun visited her four successive nights, after which she became pregnant.

and

> In the morning Estsánatlehi found a bare, flat rock and lay on it with her feet to the east, and the rising sun shone upon her. Yolkai Estsan went down where the dripping waters descended and allowed them to fall upon her. At noon the women met again on the mountaintop and Estsánatlehi said to her sister: "It is sad to be so lonesome. How can we make people so that we may have others of our kind to talk to?"

> Four days after this conversation, Yolkai Estsán said, "Elder Sister, I feel something strange moving

within me; what can it be?" And Estsánatlehi answered: "It is a child. It was for this that you lay under the waterfall. I feel, too, the motions of a child within me. It was for this that I let the sun shine upon me."

And so, Changing Woman becomes the wife of Sun to whom Nature owes her fertility. Her home is said to be in the west where each day she waits for Sun to travel across the sky. In Navajo country, which lies mostly on the Pacific Slope, rain usually comes from the west and from that direction also come the thawing breezes in the spring.

Changing Woman later gives birth to twins, Monster Slayer and Child-of-the-waters, whose feats make them the supreme war gods with power against all foreign dangers. Even so, Changing Woman stands for peace. In the Navajo pantheon Sun, Changing Woman, and The Twins form a sort of holy family, prominent in myth and ceremonial.

My thoughts turn back to Martina. What is the purpose or place of Changing Woman in Navajo life? What is it that Martina's grandmother did not want her to forget? I can only speculate. It is a Navajo belief, so I have been told, that it is better to become old gracefully than to die young; however, belief in Changing Woman's rejuvenation may delay old age. As the seasons advance she becomes old, it is true, but she has the power to reverse the process and become young again by degrees. The very name Estsánatlehi is derived by syncopation from *estsán*, woman, and *natlehi*, to change or transform.

It is also a Navajo belief that if something happened once, it may happen again. In fact, if something happened once, it is likely to happen again and maybe again and again and again. The Navajo faith in the cyclic nature of things has come to them through their direct interaction with their physical environment. And so, we return to Estsánatlehi. Earth. Mother. Changing Woman. Through her generative powers the Navajo can see themselves as an organic whole, one with the earth. Changing Woman is this personification.

> When we went in, our grandmother lay curled up, nearly killed with old age. She got up and walked with a cane of white shell to a room at the east. She came out again somewhat stronger. Then, supported by a cane of turquoise, she went into the south room. She came back walking unaided. She went next into a room at the west. She came out a young woman. She went into the north room and returned, a young girl so beautiful that we bowed our heads in wonder.

In the Navajo way, Changing Woman has a sphinxlike quality. No matter how much we know about her, the total is a question mark. She holds the mysteries of earth and the promise of fecundity. She filters vegetable dew with her skirt and carries it to thirsty fawns.

Earth goddesses dwell at the heart of every culture. They are seen equivocally as the givers and takers of life, as personification of earth, as creators of animals and vegetation. If we look back into our own cultural histories, women and earth have always been bonded. We have Gaea, Demeter, Cybele, Ishtar, Isis, Aurora, Europa, Hertha, and Eve. Where are our earth goddesses today?

A friend and I were taking a walk in Sugarhouse Park. It was early autumn and the air was cool, the kind of afternoon where clouds are rose and leaves lemon. I had just finished reading Esther Harding's *Woman's Mysteries*; the notion of women and landscape was burning in me. We became involved in a heady discussion.

"So where are our earth goddesses today?" I asked.

We reasoned and groped and argued for answers.

"Perhaps it was the Industrial Revolution that buried them," we wondered. "Or a lack of faith in unseen powers."

We circled the periphery of the park, our voices getting louder, until we almost forgot where we were.

Then, in the distance, we saw an elderly woman ripping what looked to be branches off a spruce tree.

In the midst of our discussion, here was a woman ravaging the earth! The audacity of such an act was stunning.

We walked forcefully ahead with the uncompromising zeal of missionaries, to interrogate the truth out of her.

As we drew closer we grew puzzled. The formidable figure we had seen from below now appeared benign, gentle. Her back was toward us. She was tugging at vines. I watched the veins on her gnarled hands protrude with each pull. She wore a light blue coat made of vinyl. Her hair was white, her posture bent. She turned and her face flushed innocence.

"I'm so embarrassed. You girls must find me foolish. You see, I am from Germany. When I came to this country this tree was the same age I was. We both had been replanted. Every day for twenty-seven years, I come here and watch sunsets with this tree. Now, the vines are strangling it and I come to pull them off."

My friend and I bowed our heads. After what seemed like a very long time, I managed to say, "You know, we were just talking about you, wondering where you were." The three of us pulled vines until it grew dark.

Pieces of white shell . . . remind me.

5

YUCCA

ONE NIGHT THE STARS PULLED ME INTO A DREAM. A BASKET
sat before me, coiled: around and around and around and
around. It was striped with persimmon. I should not touch
it. This much I knew. I knelt down closely and saw a
woman's long black hair curled between stitches. I picked
up a sprig of salt bush and rattled it above the hair strand.
Suddenly, the woven bowl began to pulsate, writhe, until a
snake uncoiled herself slowly. This is what I heard:

> *Sha-woman, Sha-woman, hiss*
> *Sha-woman, Sha-woman, hiss*

Tongue, rattle, hiss
Tongue, rattle, hiss
Sha-woman, Sha-woman, hiss.

She stopped. She raised her head and blew upward. I watched the breezes pull her vertically until she became a white desert torch. Yucca.

In the Navajo account of yucca's birth, Tracking Bear was a monster from whom there was no escape. He lived in a cave in the mountains. Monster Slayer, pursued by Tracking Bear, climbed a sheer wall. As he did so he grasped a fruit of the yucca in his left hand, and in his right a twig of hard oak. The monster feared these medicine rattles. Monster Slayer killed Tracking Bear and cut off his claws and large canine teeth, taking the gall and windpipe as trophies. He then cut the head into three pieces: One became the broad-leaved yucca, one the narrow-leaved yucca, and one the mescal.

And so yucca appears evenly spaced across the land. They stand as sentinels with their flowering stalks rising from vegetative swords. They are shields for creatures who live near. Sundown strikes yucca. Desert candles flame.

I remember peering into a yucca flower at dusk and seeing a tiny moth scraping pollen from within. The little white-robed pilgrim rolled the pollen into a tight ball and carried it to another blossom. There I watched her pierce the ovary wall with her long ovipositor and lay a clutch of eggs among the ovules, much as a farmer in the spring scatters seeds along his furrows. She packed the sticky mass of pollen through the openings of the stigma. Moth larvae and seeds would now develop simultaneously, with the larvae feeding on developing yucca. She walked to the edge of the petals. With her last bit of strength, she glided into the darkness, carried away by grace. The larvae would eventually gnaw their way through the ovary wall and lower themselves to the ground to pupate until the yuccas bloomed again. Circles. Cycles. Yucca and moth.

Perhaps the moth was on her way to pollinate the Navajo mind as well, for yucca and Navajo are relatives. Yucca is the single most important noncultivated plant to Indian peoples in the Southwest. It has been plaited into baskets, woven into mats, and wrapped around bundles. Early peoples walked with yucca bound around their feet. Sandals. Imagine the care extended to plants when they mean your survival.

In days of painted language, yucca leaves were soaked in warm water to soften. They were then beaten against the rocks for further pliancy. Fibers finely peeled—like corn silk, only stronger—were twisted into cordage with organic tension. This same process can be tried today with patience.

The children know yucca, *tsá'-ászi'*, intimately. On the banks of the San Juan River we stood in a circle with yucca at the center.

"What is this?" I asked.

"Yucca!" they sang out in unison.

"And what story does it tell?"

I heard as many responses as there are yucca blossoms. But one common strand connecting their stories was soap.

"We call it soapweed because there's soap under there. . . ."

"Yes?"

"Yes. You find the root under here—they pointed to the body of the plant—cut off a piece, and slice it into four strips. Then you pound it with your hands and add warm water until it lathers up."

"Then what do you do?"

"We wash our hair with the suds."

Before I knew what was happening, two boys pulled the plant out from the sand. They cut off the root, sliced it into four strips, placed it on the sandstone, and began pounding it with a rock—just as they had said. It worked: The root was frothing with suds.

The boys didn't stop there. They moved to a desert pothole that was holding rainwater. Loren bent over the basin as Bryan washed his hair. The rest of the children gathered. This was a familiar sight and they laughed.

"Loren, you better watch out—tomorrow you'll come to school with hair hanging down your back!"

The lore of yucca supports this teasing. The Navajo say a yucca shampoo will make your hair long, shiny, and black. If there are doubts as to yucca magic, just look at the children.

On another occasion, the children warned me against using yucca.

"Why not?" I asked. My curiosity was up.

"Because it might give you warts." A wave of giggles rushed over them.

But on this day, things were different. After the boys had finished their demonstration, they handed me a fresh section of the root.

"Try it."

The girls disappeared and returned with a brush they had made from a bunch of rice grass. They began combing my hair. I sat toward the wind, unable to speak.

The ritual of bathing with yucca suds is woven into the Navajo Way. It has been said that the mound of earth upon which the basket for water and suds is placed commemorates the visit of two children to Changing Woman's home, where they witnessed her rejuvenation. Blessed yucca suds have the power to transform—to change the profane to sacred, the doubtful to controlled, the contaminated to the purified.

One of the Navajo ceremonies associated with yucca washings is *Kinaaldá*, Changing Woman's puberty rites. *Kinaaldá* is part of the Blessing Way, a Navajo rite that maintains harmony for the people by attracting the goodness and power of benevolent Holy People. Most Navajo use the word *kinaaldá* to refer to the "first menses," alluding to the ceremonial rather than the physical event.

Kinaaldá ushers the adolescent Navajo girl into womanhood and invokes blessings upon her, ensuring her health, prosperity, and well-being. It is a festive occasion where the accounts of Changing Woman and her *Kinaaldá* are retold and reenacted.

The *Kinaaldá* started when White Shell Woman first menstruated. Nine days after her *Kinaaldá*, Changing Woman gave birth to twin boys: Monster Slayer and Child-of-the-waters. They were placed on the earth to kill the monsters. As soon as they had done this, their mother, Changing Woman, who was then living at Governador Knob, left and went to her home in the west, where she lives today.

After she moved to her home in the west, she created the Navajo people. When she had done this, she told these human beings to go to their original home, which was Navajo country. Before they left, she said, "After this, all the girls born to you will have periods at certain times when they become women. When the time comes, you must set a day and fix the girl up to be *Kinaaldá*; you must have these songs sung and do whatever else needs to be done at that time. After this period, a girl is a woman and will start having children.

That is what Changing Woman told the people she made in the west. She told them to go to their own country and do this.

And so *Kinaaldá* continues. A *Kinaaldá* may last anywhere from three to five days depending on the circumstances. Today, many families cannot afford this ceremony as it has become too expensive to hire a medicine man and provide food for friends and family. Even so, many young Navajo women have participated in this celebration. Traditionally, the singer or medicine man conducting the ceremony asks the mentoring woman, usually the girl's mother or aunt, to set out the basket containing the yucca roots. This is done usually before dawn of the last day of the ceremony. The roots have been carefully unearthed with two rocks found close by to aid in the crushing. The older woman ritualistically shreds the roots and pulverizes them. She then pours water into the basket, creating yucca suds so that the girl can bathe her hair. But first, the woman washes all the girl's jewelry—beads, bracelets, rings, and concha belt—and sets them on a blanket to dry. Then the girl kneels before the water, unfastens her hair tie, and begins to wash her hair with the same lather. The woman helps her, making certain she receives a good shampoo. All during the washing ritual "Songs of Dawn" are being sung and a ritual cake is being prepared.

The older woman takes the basket of soapweed water, *táláwosh*, to the west and empties it in a northerly direction. As soon as the singing stops, the young woman in

Kinaaldá wrings out her hair and begins her last run to the east before dawn. Younger sisters and friends may follow her.

The breeze coming from her as she runs
The breeze coming from her as she runs
The breeze coming from her as she runs is beautiful.

The breeze coming from her as she runs
The breeze coming from her as she runs
The breeze coming from her as she runs is beautiful.

How many times have Navajo hands asked for the release of this root from the earth? How many times have these beaten roots been rubbed between flesh in warm water until heavy lather appeared? This source of soap, containing the compound saponin, has bathed skeins of yarn and skeins of hair, leaving both to glisten in desert sunlight.

Yucca is also edible. The children call yucca fruit "Navajo bananas." When boiled, it tastes much like summer squash, slightly sweet but with a twist of bitterness. But most of the yucca fruit is left in the heat to dry and wither. I have cut into its flesh many times and found exquisite symmetry. Six windows—once panes for seeds—become a chartreuse kaleidoscope.

The children look through yucca and see each other playing the ball and stick game, traditionally known as the "moccasin game."

"You play the game like this," they said. "You make a ball out of the yucca root with your hands, then everyone takes off their shoes and lines them up on either side of the yucca. One side takes the ball and hides it inside one of the shoes. The other team has to guess which shoe it's in. If they guess right it's their turn to hide the ball, but if they're wrong, the other side gets to cut off a yucca leaf. The side with the most yucca sticks at the end of the game wins."

Another story is told. A long, long time ago all creatures on earth, including insects, spoke as human beings. The Animal People gathered around the yucca and said, "Let's have a shoe game." A great hoopla rose from the crowd as everyone showed his favor for such an event.

"But how will we keep score?" asked a small beast.

"We will use the blades of yucca as counters," spoke another. And one hundred and two yucca sticks were pulled. A ball from the root of yucca was shaped, along with a stick for pointing.

"We will have the shoe game at a place called Tse'yaa Hodilhil," they said. And everyone ran, jumped, flew and crawled to the designated site.

Gopher dug two shallow furrows on either side. Four moccasins were placed in each groove and then covered with sand. Then it was asked among the herds, swarms, and flocks, "What shall we bet?"

A great stirring occurred in the animal assemblage as everyone offered opinions. Finally, all the diurnal beings said, "We will bet the earth to have continual sunlight."

The nocturnal beings stepped forward and said, "We will bet the sky to have perpetual darkness."

And so the bets were placed between day and night.

There were many, many Animal People on both sides. The diurnal creatures on the south, the nocturnal creatures on the north. Anticipation for the contest grew like midsummer corn.

The game began with one side hiding the ball in one of the four moccasins, then covering the moccasins up with sand. The other side began guessing with the indicator stick which shoe the ball was in. They were given three chances. If they guessed correctly it became their turn to hide the ball. If they were fooled, the opponents took a yucca counter. Back and forth, back and forth it went, with lots of laughter and singing.

The Animal People became so immersed in the shoe game that no one realized morning had come. They continued to play throughout the day and into the night placing their bets high, with neither side ever quite winning all one hundred and two yucca sticks.

They did things then just as people do today. Once they started something, they would not stop. The wager between day and night still continues.

The shoe game is played by Navajos with delight. Some call it Navajo gambling. But those who know the stories say it keeps Sun and Moon in balance.

After all the children have shared their own versions of the game, they are quick to tell you that "you must only play this game in winter." A botanist will tell you winter is the dormant season for yucca. Earth wisdom.

I brought out my pouch and took a slice, a circle of yucca. It had been aged by Sun. Once supple, now shriveled. Bitter, hard. What could this be? I mused over the possibilities. If I were home, it could be cucumber, zucchini, even eggplant. But here it could be peyote or datura, any number of powerful medicines. Where could they take me? I closed my eyes and slipped the yucca slice into my mouth. From a far-off place I could smell the smoke of piñyon.

Yucca. Plants. Navajo. Plants yield their secrets to those who know them. They can weep the colors of chokecherry tears, purplish-brown, into a weaver's hands. They can be backbones for baskets holding the blessings of *Kinaaldá*. Cedar bark and sage can purify; Indian paintbrush soothes an ailing stomach. Juniper ash water creates blue cornmeal. Petals of larkspur are sprinkled in ceremony. Native plants are a repository. They hold our health. A Navajo medicine man relies on plants as we rely on pharmacies.

Edward S. Ayensu, director of the Office of Biological Conservation at the Smithsonian Institution, tells a story about an African herbalist who told his students to pay attention to the natural world, to listen and observe the behavior of animals such as lizards, snakes, birds, rodents, and insects.

To stress his point, the herbalist narrated a fight between two chameleons. As Ayensu describes it:

> At the climax of the fight one of the chameleons passed out. The other quickly dashed into a thicket and came back with a piece of a leaf in its mouth. It forcibly pushed the leaf into the mouth of the unconscious lizard. In a matter of two or three minutes the defeated chameleon shook its body and took off.
>
> The specific plant that saved the life of the chameleon was not disclosed to me. When I insisted on knowing, the teacher smiled and said, "This is a trade secret. It is a plant that can spring a dying person to life. Unless you became one of us I cannot tell you."

This is earth medicine, and it is all around us, delivered into the hands that trust it. What do we know?

Yucca. The desert torch burns and returns its ashes to crimson sand. A snake slithers across the way and recoils itself under a slickrock slab. This is what I heard:

> *Sha-woman, Sha-woman, hiss*
> *Sha-woman, Sha-woman, hiss*
> *Tongue, rattle, hiss*
> *Tongue, rattle, hiss*
> *Sha-woman, Sha-woman, hiss.*

Silence. A basket sits before me, coiled: around and around and around and around. It is striped with persimmon.

A BOUQUET
OF FEATHERS
· BOUND
BY YARN

Birds. A bouquet of feathers bound by yarn. If I offer them to Sun and push off with my mind, can I then know flight? Each one of these feathers is a gift. A plume of power. A lesson. I never know when I will find one or where, much less from whom. But suddenly it appears, as though the individual bird says, "Here I am."

I was in search of Great Horned Owl. I knew she lived in the eastern stand of cottonwoods. Her nest was still visible; summer leaves had not blocked it from the sky. I crossed barbed wire fences, waded through streams, and ultimately trespassed on Old Man Spark's land. For some reason I had to establish eye contact with Owl. I could feel I was getting close, or perhaps I was just tired—wishing Owl's grace would befall me. Then, I saw her. She flew. So quiet and elegant, she drifted over the meadow. Low. With a tempered upswing, she landed in an aspen. I had to look twice to make sure she was there as the grey-tawny feathers merged with the tree. Yes, she was. I could not be content with the distance between us. But as I contemplated my next move she left, as efficaciously as she had appeared. Gone.

I entered the forest that she had slipped into. Shadows grew. Sounds became amplified. A snap of a twig put my nerves on edge. I felt cornered. For a fleeting moment I caught myself, perhaps in the river's reflection. This was too contrived. I was leaving Owl no space. My simple wish had become an intrusion, typical of my intensity.

Give it up, I said to myself. Be grateful for what you saw—

So I released myself. The chase was off. I turned around and walked back to the meadow.

It was a splendid afternoon. Lupine and yarrow were woven between grasses; swallowtails connected flower to flower. My eyes scanned the glade until I noticed a break in the tapestry. What I took to be a brown leaf was a feather: Owl's. I reached down and picked it up. My fingers ran across its webbing. It was velveteen. By letting go of my obsession I had found her path. Not wanting to make more of this, I quietly kept on walking, respectfully listening for such nuances as where the small birds' voices waxed and waned. I changed direction. It was a pleasure to walk so intuitively. A few feet ahead I could see another feather—this time from the breast of Owl. It was fine, transparent, with hints of striping. I held it up in the air. Sunlight filtered through. The wind sneaked up from behind me and snatched the feather from my fingers. I followed. Slowly the feather drifted south, then fell. I picked it up and let the wind take it where it might—again and again and again. Finally I picked it off a wild rose at the edge of the meadow. I looked up and, simply, stood before her, Great Horned Owl.

We spent the better part of a day together. She was always aware of my presence and I hers, but we went about our business, as one does in the company of friends.

In the Navajo Way, Owl and Eagle are the transformed children of the Tsé Bit'a'i monsters. Monster Slayer charged them so that they would never harm earth people, would live absolutely without any meanness in them. He told Owl, "In days to come men will listen to your voice and know what will be their future: Sometimes you will tell the truth and sometimes you will lie."

The story continues:

> After Monster Slayer had completed his business with nothing more to do, he was determined to go home. Unfortunately, he soon found there was no way for him to descend the rock. Nothing but a winged creature could reach or leave the ledge on which he stood.
>
> As he gazed across the land below him, he noticed Bat Woman walking along near the base of the cliff.
>
> "Grandmother," he called. "Please come and rescue me from this cliff."
>
> "Hush, boy, and be patient," she answered as she hid behind a rock. Again she came into view, and again he begged her to carry him down, but she gave the same reply. This happened three times.

When she appeared for the fourth time, Monster Slayer pleaded, "I will give you the feathers of *Tse'na'hale* if you will take me off this rock." When Bat Woman heard this, she approached the base of the rock, then disappeared under the ledge where he stood.

Suddenly he heard a strange flapping sound and a voice calling to him: "Shut your eyes. You must not see how I ascend."

He did what he was told, and the next thing he knew Bat Woman stood behind him.

"Climb into this basket and I will carry you down," she said.

"Grandmother," he said, "I am afraid to enter your basket as the strings it hangs on are as thin as a spider's web."

"Have no fear," she replied. "I have carried deer in this basket many times. The strings are strong enough to bear you."

With Bat Woman's assurance, Monster Slayer climbed into her basket and was safely transported to earth.

Together they plucked the two *Tse'na'hale* and put the feathers in her basket. Monster Slayer kept only one large wing feather from each of the birds as his trophies. He warned Bat Woman, upon her travels, not to take the path of the giant sunflowers, or something unpredictable might happen. Despite his warning, that is exactly where she walked.

She had not taken many steps among the sunflowers when she heard a fluttering sound behind her. A little bird of a peculiar appearance flew past her close to her ear. The more steps she took, the more fluttering she heard—with more and more birds of varying plumages flying over her shoulder in every direction.

Bat Woman was astonished. She had never seen such extraordinary colored feathers before. She looked all around her until, suddenly, she noticed that all the birds were flying out of her own basket. She tried to hold them in, to catch them as they flew out, but her actions were in vain.

Finally she laid down her basket and watched helplessly. Her feathers changed into little birds of all kinds—wrens, warblers, titmice, and the like—flying away until her basket was empty. Thus it was that the little birds were created.

Birds color Navajoland like a living rainbow. According to the Diné, in fact, rainbows get their colors from being lined with feathers. So often, I have sat on the desert with voluminous clouds encircling me and watched an arched prism with wings span the basin.

The Navajo refer to birds as fliers or *naa'a'ii*. I have also heard the children call them *tsidii*. My favorite of The People's names for birds is "the airborne"—birds soaring on heated air currents, full and exuberant. Close your eyes and see the sun splitting light through a red-tailed hawk's russet feathers. Or imagine the delicate hoverings of kestrels.

The naming and classification of birds in the Navajo Way reflects perception and thoughtful observation. Categories tend to focus on the religious rather than the scientific.

Examples of Navajo nomenclature include marsh hawk, named *ch'il taat'agii*, meaning One-flying-close-to-the-woods; mountain chickadee, referred to as *ch'ishiibeezhii*, which describes its call; flicker is known as *at'a'hayaachii* or Wing-area-under-red. And the family of swallows is identified as táshchozhii or "water-players." Each of these creates an environmental picture based on either behavior, song, or color.

I speculate over some of the Anglo nomenclature of birds: Wilson's snipe, Forster's tern, Swainson's thrush, Lewis's woodpecker, Townsend's warbler, LeConte's sparrow, and even "common" egret: What natural images do these names conjure up in our minds? What integrity do we give back to the bird with our labels?

If we will sit for a while, allow entire afternoons to pass in the presence of birds, we may find they are skilled in subtle pedagogy. Courage is the lesson of killdeer as it feigns a broken wing to protect its young. Tenaciousness is the coot who tries again and again to fly. White pelicans are cooperative fishermen as they corral their prey in self-made circles. Bittern is patience hidden in the marsh. Solitude is the curlew who evades civilization. A prairie falcon's prowess will split doves above the desert. Wildness is the raven. Ingenuity belongs to the kinglet who entices insects with its ruby crown. Starlings speak of survival. Robins are the blessings of being average. While sparrows prosper in their anonymity.

Birds and animals within the Navajo mind acquire mythic stature. They are approached in both nature and story as possessing those qualities inherent yet greatly magnified. For example:

> . . . the white might take the vulture for a repulsive
> bird not worth contemplating, where the Indian saw
> a creature who never drank a drop of water, and
> whose eyesight was keener than any other bird's.

An effort to concentrate intensely on the vulture's power might get a small war party safely through open desert country.

This same type of respect or understanding is expressed through the taboos that accompany flora and fauna. Franc Newcomb describes some of these practices.

It is a Navajo belief that every form of animal or plant life on the face of the earth belongs to the god that created that particular plant or animal and gave it life; therefore, human beings have no right to use or destroy any part of this creation without permission from the creator.

Similarly,

In the Navajo religion, each small form of life is accorded a proportionate spiritual status, ceremonial respect, and economic importance as that given to any of the greater forms of creation. Worms, insects, beetles, and birds are all protected by as stringent taboos as are the buffalo, the coyote, and the bear. None of these things, large or small, may be killed unless there is some special purpose or reason for the killing; and then certain rites or prayers must accompany the act to guard against a possibility of evil results.

Birds specifically are associated with various practices, omens, and taboos. Within Navajo cosmology there are guidelines:

"Never kill a bird." "Never eat the flesh of a bird." The Navajo reservation is a veritable bird sanctuary because many members of its feathered population are considered sacred and others are accredited with evil powers so that all are protected by very stringent taboos. Any form of life that wears feathers or possesses wings that spread like a fan are associated with the winds, the clouds, and the various forms of moisture. The wing of the dragonfly, the wing of the moth, or the spread tail of the bird are all cloud symbols, and transversely, the small cirrus clouds are called the feathers of the rainbird. The symbol of the summer thunderstorm is a bird with spread wings from which rain and lightning descend.

There are many birds whose cries are supposed to call for rain. The most common of these are the quail, the killdeer, the snipe, and the plover. Yellow birds and blue birds are respected because of their coloring, as yellow is the color symbol of pollen, while blue indicates summer skies, abundant vegetation (green and blue have the same ceremonial significance), ripe corn, and turquoise. Birds whose feathers are flecked with white are said to have been marked by water-spray or foam, which is termed "water pollen." This association with water gives these birds partial control over certain forms of moisture. Some birds are sacred because they were given charge of the wildflowers, and grass seed, and the grains.

Birds are sacred. They are harbingers of spring as well as augurs of evil. Ritual surrounds them. One has only to have spent brief moments with birds in spring to know of their own sense of ritual. I have spent hours watching sandhill cranes flock to fertile meadows and dance. Courtship. With outstretched wings, they engage themselves in deep bows to one another, then move to bounding leaps, with each long leg extending out then in, out then in. And what about the rock wren who makes a path of pebbles leading to its nest? Or the strutting grouse who displays for a female?

The Navajo term *nahaghá* is translated to mean ritual. This labels a large and significant category of Navajo behavior that non-Navajos least understand. The primary function of all Navajo ritual is to maintain or restore *hózhó*.

There is a phrase spoken by the Navajo—*Sạ'ah naagháii bik'eh hózhó*—which roughly translates into their expression of happiness, health, the beauty of earth, and the harmony of their relations with others. *Sạ'ah naagháii* represents the capacity of all life and living things to achieve immortality through reproduction or perpetuation of the species. *Sạ'ah* denotes the verb usage "to grow, or mature." The propagation of the Navajo People is founded upon growth, or emergence from four preceding worlds, each evolution shedding darkness and gaining more light and refinement, thus enabling them to come closer to the universal whole, to beauty or *hózhó*. *Bik'eh hózhó* represents the peace and harmony essential to the perpetuation of all living species.

Rituals are the formulas by which harmony is restored. They are symbolic actions born of the Navajo mythic reality. Donald Sandner elaborates:

> By means of origin myths and cosmogonic myths, a picture is built up of what the world is, how it came to be, and how it may be expected to function in the future. It makes no difference whether the facts on which this world view are founded are true or not.

The myth makes do with what "facts" it has, and goes on about its business of creating an intuitive emotional interpretation of them. The rituals embody sacred action appropriate to the structure of the world built up by the myths. They go hand in hand, completing and complementing each other— the mythic reality and the ritual response.

Clyde Kluckhohn maintains:

The Navaho notion is that the universe works according to rules. If one can discover the rules and follow them, he may remain safe or be restored to safety.

. . . Navahos accept nature and adapt themselves to her demands as best they can, but they are not utterly passive, not completely the pawns of nature. They do a great many things that are designed to control nature physically and to repair damage caused by the elements. But they do not ever hope to master nature. For the most part The People try to influence her with various songs and rituals. . . .

Given their view of the world as expressed in the symbols of language and ritual, the Navajo find ritual behavior not only appropriate but necessary to their personal well-being and survival. A Navajo not only feels he should follow certain observances and avoid others; he finds it dangerous to do otherwise.

Personal ritual or shared ceremony rooted in landscape provides connections, continuity. It reminds us that we do not stand alone. Rather, we become initiated into something much larger than ourselves. We experience a universal embrace. This is not exclusive to Navajo people. We all share in a cosmic celebration. It may be as subtle as noting the full moon or as concrete a commitment as bathing in the Ganges River.

If we participate in our own rituals, we are exercising faith, a trust in unseen powers.

Birds and Navajo. Dance and ritual. I saw these elements merging together at a powwow in Lukachukai. So often dance, as we know it, is a means of entertainment or personal performance. At a powwow, dance becomes an expression of personal identity. Tribal roots are reaffirmed and explored, individually as well as collectively. On this summer night, I caught a glimpse of the "Native American mind" through dance.

We followed the red cliffs that act as a backbone for Lukachukai, Arizona. As we drove into town, first impressions were of dust and heat, unyielding heat, with temperatures so high I surrendered to the possibility of watching my blood boil. We stopped at the gas station for a cool drink. On the window was a sign: POWWOW AT THE RODEO GROUNDS, JULY 15, 1979—8:00 P.M. We decided to attend. Feelings of inadequacy crept in, embarrassment, as we drove to the celebration. We don't belong. Are Anglos shunned? For heaven's sake, don't take photographs.

We gave our tickets to the woman at the gate. Even my *yá'át'ééh* did not come out right. Beads of anxiety gathered around my temples. At least my hair is dark. There must be over five hundred Indian people here—and seven white. We moved among the crowd and then I left the people I was with. I felt more comfortable alone. There is strength in solitude. Feelings of anticipation filled me as I forgot myself and became absorbed in the occasion.

Families and friends gathered. Participants and dancers were getting ready as a circle of pickup trucks with tailgates pointed outwards created the arena. Colors—all around.

The Sunshield Singers began. Young men singing high-pitched chants. Eyes closed as they sang to the heavens. Vibrant. Virile. Central Singers joined in. Older men singing a lower pitch. Slower, much slower, like deep, deep drums. I felt a wisdom and sadness emerge from their repetition. And then darkness.

The dancing began! Skins, feathers, bones, shells, beads, claws, paint, and brightly colored fabrics. Shields, rattles, fans, sashes, breastplates, headdresses, moccasins, and jewelry. Each dancer a dream figure, proud and provocative. Together they walked slowly in a circle, chests high, chins lifted. I sat in awe, feeling as though I was being taken into an ancient trance. Colored circles, drums, and chants.

The men danced first in a War Dance. One man wore a porcupine headdress with two eagle feathers dangling from the nape of his neck. A breastplate of bones covered his torso, bucksin leggings and moccasins his legs and feet. An array of feathers attached to the small of his back gave him the aura of flight. He danced hard and deliberately. In circles. The singers' pace quickened, their pitch rose. I never saw him lose his focus. His eyes penetrated the seductive night, looking up, looking down. With each beat his spirit danced. My heart took on his cadence.

Then it was the women's turn. Four young women in the Shawl Dance. They swirled and spun, swirled and spun. Circular motions kept them in one place. With heads and backs low, their arms encircled the air around them with their shawls, now capes creating a canopy above them. I imagined great egrets with plumes, circling their nests before landing. Their small feet followed the murmur of earth and drums, earth and drums, their moccasins attuned to female rhythms. Their faces were burnished and bright. Swirls. More swirls. Soft swirls. Their shawls, the four sacred colors: red, yellow, blue, and black. In their dance was the evocation of life. I felt my mother's presence.

Finally, the children danced, unabashed, and joyful. Yet the power of tradition calmed them as they tried so hard to concentrate on the drums, on their feet. Still, in the children's eyes I saw smiles. For a small part of an evening they became the stuff shamans are made of: with an archetypal eye that bears the past and the future in its vision.

The powwow ended with all people walking in a circle to the voice of the drums, to the voice of the drums, to the voice of the drums. It seemed as though hundreds of listening feet were walking to the voice of the drums. I wanted to join them.

As I hold this bouquet of feathers bound by yarn, I unleash them. Millions of colored birds burst into song.

7

COYOTE FUR

I have a friend, Valdez Tom, who grew up on the Navajo Reservation. He was attending the University of Utah on a government grant for an undergraduate degree in premed. As I was leaving Salt Lake for his home, I asked him if there was anything I should watch for.

"Yes," he said. "Watch for Coyote." He laughed and then grew very serious. "Watch out for Coyote." His black eyes were piercing. I told him I would.

We were camped just outside Montezuma Creek, Utah, on a high bluff overlooking Hovenweep. Deep arroyos cut into the desert skin. The water that usually flowed there was absent now because of scorching temperatures and drought. The arroyos became our paths.

Tall tamarisks grew on either side, making it difficult to see. Branches pushed aside by the hiker ahead snapped back at me like whips.

I fantasized a small machete to ease my way, but then felt guilty as a cluster of delicate mauve blossoms stared up at me. Desert heather.

I was nervous. I'll be honest. Each step I took brought me closer to the imaginary rattles of Big Snake.

"You've been reading too much," my companion said. "Loosen up. Those things belong in the minds of children."

How could I tell him the mind creates those things that exist. I couldn't, and so I concentrated on birdlife to avoid a confrontation. After several hours of walking (our canvas boots had turned pink), we stopped to sit on some boulders. To the west, on the horizon, heatwaves danced in front of a large blue mountain.

Sleeping Indian. They say he will rise again with the power of The People.

I could see the mountain take the form of a sleeping warrior: headdress, strong profile, inflated chest, arms folded at the waist; then long, long legs extending northward. Somehow I felt reassured by his presence and never doubted the day native breath would blow into him.

A warm wind rushed through the bottom of the canyon. Cottonwoods trembled. The wind delivered a reprieve from the pelting rays of the sun and biting no-see-ums. Then, just as the breeze lifted, I caught sight of a lone coyote. Thoughts of Valdez's warning came to mind, then vanished as my eyes feasted on the elegant creature. I felt warned not to look, but the temptation and luxury were too great. I would pay whatever consequences, but later.

From the rim of the canyon, Coyote's slow, steady gait looked deliberate and direct. Perhaps he was following a scent. He stopped. I thought I saw his eyes squinting at the sun. Beautiful, he was not at all scraggly as the cartoonists would have you believe. Regal. Proud. Intelligent. His chest was the color of ochre, as were the insides of his ears; the body was silver-grey; a black line ran perfectly centered down his tail, like a burn, concentrating at the tip—never had I seen such a plume of fur. His face remained still, slightly raised. I could see black character lines outlining his eyes, nose, and mouth. He stood there for some time. I was starting to take him for granted. My eyes wandered. Gone. We lost him. For a few seconds I thought I could see his feet moving beneath the big sage he must have been traveling through, but that was probably just my imagination. Coyote mirage.

That night I made my bed on a slab of slickrock. I spent an eerie night among nocturnal cries and shrieks. The desert awakens with the sunset and is hushed by dawn. Bobcat, Great Horned Owl, and a mysterious "yap-yap" bird all taunted the darkness. Cooper's Hawk was perched above me, and toads tried my nerves as their chants became a mantra that my pulse took on. Were these allies of Coyote? What was the price I must pay? I was dazzled by the Milky Way until it, too, seemed to turn against me, becoming one million pairs of eyes. Then, coming up from the Hovenweep ruins, I heard drums.

Boom-ba-boom, boom, boom. Boom-ba-boom, boom, boom. My throat tightened, and I held my breath so as not to mistake my heartbeat for the *boom-ba-boom, boom, boom. Boom-ba-boom, boom, boom.*

Anasazi Drums. They continued until the sun rose. *Boom-ba-boom, boom* . . . Then, silence. Nothing. No sound. No movement. Nothing.

For some time now, I have tried to explain rationally where these nocturnal beats originated, but to no avail. River cobbles? No river. A powwow? No people for miles around. As a last resort, I approached an old woman who was the grandmother of a child I was teaching. I explained the sounds and the circumstances to her, and she smiled and said, "You heard what you heard."

The next morning I hiked out of the canyon alone. In the middle of the trail lay a fresh pile of Coyote dung. A golden scarab crawled out.

I am wary of this piece of fur in my hand, fur pulled gently by the fingers of sage as Coyote misjudged the spaces between them. He is lean. He will survive us. Ma'ii, as the Navajo call him, is the Trickster. His origin occurred, it is told, when The People had not been in the fourth world long. Suddenly they saw Sky bend down and Earth rise up, touching for only a brief moment. As that connection was made, Coyote sprang forth.

Coyote is paradox personified. His ambiguous nature, evasive qualities, and adaptability keep him at the center of Navajo folklore. He lives outside of time, immune to mortal mores. He brings with him a restlessness, which is perhaps unconsciously necessary to an agricultural, stable people. He enables them to enjoy the sense of relief that comes from being able to laugh at oneself. Coyote frees them from cultural restrictions as they break taboos vicariously. Yet at the same time, Coyote is a form of cultural affirmation.

Trickster can be both profane and sacred, a bumbler and a hero. He lives somewhere between nature and culture; order and chaos; animal, human, and god. He cannot be killed as he even pushes the boundaries of life and death. Coyote is the embodiment of possibility, the split between creativity and the unknown. He eludes us.

Coyote knows many stories. From his mouth stories foam and froth, spilling over his sparkling teeth. He will drop anything to woo you with his breath. He is intoxicating and his stories are delicious. Coyote is a *raconteur*. He knows how to save the lives of his children.

Coyote tales nurture Navajo life. "The old men used to tell these stories when we were young so that we would think," one individual explained, "but only between the first frost and the last thaw." Stories are continually being spun on long winter nights inside the hogans. These stories not only educate the children, but amuse as well. Coyote transcends The People and allows them to live beyond their means.

COYOTE ENTERTAINS PORCUPINE

Coyote visited Porcupine and found him sitting in his home working hard at something. Coyote asked what he was doing and Porcupine told him that he was making something that later on might be useful.

Coyote asked four times how the thing Porcupine was making could help him to earn a living. But Porcupine would not tell him, and without saying any more built a fire. He took some piñon bark from his summer hogan and put it on the charcoal in the fire. The bark turned into tenderloin. He gave this meat to Coyote and Coyote ate it.

Coyote invited Porcupine to come to his home within four days. When Porcupine arrived Coyote was making something. Porcupine wanted to know what Coyote was making, but Coyote behaved in the same manner as Porcupine and refused to tell him anything. Porcupine asked four times, but Coyote said nothing. Coyote built a fire and pulled some piñon bark from the roof of his house. He put this on the charcoal in the fire. But instead of turning to meat the bark just caught fire and turned to ashes. Coyote did not know what to do; he went outside and did not return. After a while Porcupine went home.

During the course of many months, Coyote and Porcupine kept visiting each other. Each time Porcupine prepared something delicious for Coyote to eat; the first time he placed bark into the fire and it turned to tenderloin. The second time he threw sumac into the fire and it became prairie dogs. The third time he shot an arrow into the fire and it turned into a fat, juicy intestine. And the fourth time he sprinkled sumac once again over the fire and it popped into a blood-stuffed intestine.

Coyote attempted these same tricks; the result was always ashes.

Coyote hides behind bushes and leaves poisoned bait for you to suck on. He is foul. He has even been known to wear his penis on his back, twelve feet long, in search of love. But don't worry, he will revive you. He will present you with a mirror when no one is looking and make you wild with laughter!

Coyote is a border figure, always on the fringe of society. Typically, Trickster has no home, so he sets his devious mind to play. Another animal helpmate is solicited to do his work. Badger. As Coyote sends Badger in myriad directions to meet all of his requirements for home building, Coyote enjoys the life of leisure. He makes high-level demands, yet shows an inability to make decisions. His thoughts are both organized and chaotic. He has vision, but no follow-through. After all of Badger's tasks have been completed, and the way is clear for Coyote to proceed with his plans to erect his new home, he fails, only to live in a mound of dirt forever. The bumbler. The wanderer. Things never quite work out as Trickster imagines.

Who turns Coyote's mind? Just about the time you have lost your faith, Coyote restores it, emerging as a cultural hero—the other end of his character spectrum. First Man and First Woman were worried about The People being cold. Winter was around the corner and the only fire available to them was in the clutch of the monsters. With ingenuity and spirit, Coyote assured the crowd he could outsmart and overcome Big Fly and Fire-god who reigned on top of the smoldering mountain. After Flicker and Hawk failed in their attempt to retrieve fire (thus becoming Red-shafted Flicker and Red-tailed Hawk), First Woman tied a special flask to the end of Coyote's tail. He took with him a bag of salt crystals and seashells. As he approached the fly-monsters who were standing guard over the flames, he gave them offerings of white shell to divert their attention. Then in a split second, he hurled the salt crystals into their millions of eyes, grabbed some fire, placed it in his container, and ran down the mountain to The People. First Woman had warned him of running in a straight line, so as Fire-god threw bolts of lightning down upon him, he ran in a zigzag pattern to miss the attacks. Just as the fire began to singe the hair on his tail, Squirrel untied the flask. Everyone cheered. Coyote had brought fire to the world!

Coyote can also be a soothsayer. When The People arrived in the fourth world after journeying upward through a reed, Coyote said this:

> "Let me divine your fate." Coyote picked up a stone, and said, "If it sinks we perish; if it floats we live," and he threw it into the water. It sank, of course, and all were angry with him and reviled him but he answered them saying: "If we all live, and continue to increase as we have done, the earth will soon be too small to hold us, and there will be no room for the cornfields. It is better that each of us should live but a time on this earth and then leave and make room for our children." They saw the wisdom of his words and were silent.

There is, however, a darker side to this character. Coyote is also aligned with "skinwalkers." Through witchcraft, skinwalkers explain for the Navajo things that would otherwise be left as unknowns: death, sickness, bad dreams, and ill luck. They report in darkness, always prowling between dusk and dawn; if seen, it is a sure sign trouble awaits you.

The exact description of skinwalkers is unclear. Some Navajo believe it is Coyote; others say they are half-human, half-wolf—equivalent to European werewolves. Barry Lopez supports this notion in his book *Of Wolves and Men*:

> The Navajo word for wolf, *mai-oh*, is a synonym for witch. . . . A Navajo witch becomes a werewolf by donning a wolfskin. If he means to kill someone, he travels to his hogan at night, climbs up on the roof, and tosses something through the smokehole to

make the fire flare, revealing where people are sleeping. He then pushes down a poison on the end of a stick, which the victim inhales. (Dirt rolling off the roof at night is a sign that a werewolf is about.) . . . In addition to killing people, Navajo werewolves raided graveyards and mutilated bodies.

This tradition is very much alive on the reservation today. When the sun goes down, stories of skinwalkers rise. Tales of mangled sheep, automobile accidents, missing children—any sort of unexplainable act falls under their domain. Owls may whisper warnings, snakes may tremble of a sickness foretold, but a Navajo witch is the undoing of harmony. Coyote walks upright wearing smoked medicine bundles around his hips.

The Navajo children I know speak of skinwalkers with authority, but never without caution. Their voices lower and at times become very somber. One boy, Alvin, told of a night when he sneaked out of his hogan and saw four skinwalkers standing around the fire with their backs turned. He painted a scene of hairy figures conspiring with blue flames.

Another account was given by a child who warned, "The skinwalkers come and make an X with their chalk on the door of your family home. It will not come off. They are telling you something bad is going to happen."

I would never question the power of Navajo witches. At times, I thought I was being choked by them. If one has ever driven the long, lonely stretches of night in Navajo country, these stories are not so foreign. Your mind travels back and forth from the real and the imagined. After a while, they become one and the same. A creature crosses in front of your car. You stop and get out for a closer look.

You find nothing—not even footprints. You get back into your car and discover you are driving in the opposite direction.

Each personal account brings word back to The People that skinwalkers still roam the night and ravage interiors. Coyote howls. Doors shut.

Coyote's ceremonial name, Atse'xa ke', is translated to mean First Warrior. In the past, warriors seeing a coyote on the trail ahead of them would turn back rather than take the chance his appearance portends. One night some Navajos from Fort Sumner were on a Comanche raid:

> . . . while they were asleep, a coyote walked into camp. Although they offered prayers and made jewel deposits, the bad luck still held. Four of the part were killed; and the rest, who scattered, were lucky to get home alive.

Coyote was last seen on the Southwest desert, trotting briskly over tiny offerings of corn pollen left on his behalf.

8

A
BONE
FROM
BLACK MOUNTAIN

NOT FAR FROM WHERE I PICKED UP THE PIECE OF COYOTE
fur lay a tiny bone. A fibula. Perhaps it belongs to Jackrabbit, Gahtsoh. I have been told that among the Navajo,
Jackrabbit is considered a doctor because he has brought
The People through starvation. Since Jackrabbit eats valu-
able herbs, the Navajo believe the entire animal should be
eaten and nothing wasted. It is also customary that when a
rabbit is killed, the bones of its hind legs must be broken
by the hunter. Then those who receive the meat know it
has been freshly killed and not found dead, taken by an
eagle or hawk.

I hold this bone in my hand and turn it carefully. I

wonder how this little creature met death. The fibula is whole; my suspicion lies in the talons of a raptor. I dream of having days to carve long, delicate swirls around this calcium tube. The Gahtsoh wind-spirit has long since fled, but I would carve its stories. I would hollow out pink marrow and leave it as an offering to beetles. Then I would begin my trek to Black Mountain to stand tall on its highest ridge and prepare myself for what was about to come. Take full sweeping breaths. Inhale. Exhale. Inhale. Exhale. I would exert my whole body until I was a feather being blown upward by the wind. Then, when the sun settled just so, I would take this rabbit whistle, now a platinum reed, and I would blow and blow and blow and blow; four times, until all the Animal People gathered beneath its shrill cry. Then would I shrink into the body of Flea and listen to the stories they tell around Black Mountain.

On one such evening a gathering occurred. It was winter. Moon was being eclipsed by Earth and all the desert sang epithalamium.

Bear—Shash, Mountain Lion—Náshdóítsoh, Coyote—Ma'ii, Badger—Nahasch'id, Skunk—Gólízhii, Porcupine—Dahsání, Squirrel—Haazeitsoh, Chipmunk—Haazeists'osi, Beaver—Chaa'baghani, Prairie Dog—Dlǫ́ǫ́, and Collared Lizard—Na'ashą́'ii doot'izhí—all were there. And so were the Bird People and the Insect People, along with Deer Woman, Big Snake, Black-god and Begochidi, the Great Hunter. They assembled together to witness Earth paint the full, white face of Moon in ceremony. It was a gathering of faith. All looked upward as the Milky Way sent streamers of stars shooting east and west on their behalf.

"These are our parents," said Shash. "The shadow on

Moon's face is the curve of our Mother. The orange glow is illumination from our Father. Our conception is in them. By accepting their gift tonight, we honor the givers. Let us recall who we are." And then Shash told the following story:

"As you all know, I am guardian of Sun's house. But as you also know, I have walked the line with darkness. Black Mountain is my home. Tonight is a good night to tell you of my origins.

I was once known as Changing-bear-maiden. I was beautiful and highly desirable. I was greatly respected and talented. All things were in my circle of possibilities. I was a maiden who despised men and made conditions of matrimony so difficult no man could fulfill them.

I had brothers and they were very happy with my arrangement, for I was a model housekeeper and did many chores for them. One day, however, the wind blew rumors of Coyote lust. My brothers caught word of this through the fingers of cottonwood trees. They warned me of this danger, but I was too arrogant for alarm.

By and by, Coyote presented his best self to me. He made marriage look very attractive. Still, I avoided his requests and resisted his temptations. I practiced all the lore I had been given and even made Coyote kill Big Monster and undergo death four times. Finally, I could take no more. I had reached the end of coquetry. Coyote's gentle nature softened me and I yielded to him, discovering for myself how nice it was to have a husband."

Squirrel, who knows everything that goes on in the forest because of his lofty perch whispered to the others:

From the moment Coyote was allowed to crawl under the fringe of her robe, she was in his power.

> . . . Into a clean, harmonious household wandered
> impurity, filth, and disorder . . . then the horrible
> potentialities of the beautiful girl began to come out.

Coyote, in the background snickered. His eyes glistened in
the shadows.

"My passion for Coyote grew as did my brothers' op-
position," continued Shash. "They told me I would change,
that it would come slowly like the interface of seasons, that
I would not recognize the transformation until winter was
upon me. This was true. I grew a long muzzle, capable of
breaking a person's neck. (Oh, that I had broken Coyote's
. . .) My teeth became a collection of bone awls that I
gathered from the children of enemies. And long, coarse
hair began to grow on my hands, arms, and legs, eventually spreading over my entire body."

"With the exception of your breasts, Shash-maiden!"
jeered Coyote from behind the pinyon.

"My story is almost through," assured Shash to the others. "My brother found me in the heat of the afternoon. He
raised his voice to the level of Jays and said:

> You shall live again, but no longer as this mischiev-
> ous maiden. You shall live in other forms, so you
> may be of service to your kind and not a thing of
> evil.

He cut off my head and said: 'Let us see if in another
life you will do better. . . .' He then threw my head at the
foot of a pinyon tree and I emerged as you see me now."

All the animals cooed and ahhed.

"Can this be so?" said the entire village of Prairie Dogs.

"Wait," said Shash. "There is more. . . ."

"My brother then cut off the nipples of Changing-bear-maiden and said to them:

> Had you belonged to a good woman and not to a
> foolish witch, it might have been your luck to suckle
> men. Yours were of no use to your kind, but now
> I shall make you of use in another form.

He threw the nipples up into a pinyon tree, heretofore fruitless, and they became edible pine nuts!"

"Bless you, Shash!" sang all the Bird People. Not only are you our mentor on Black Mountain, you provided us with food."

Shash's coat glistened in the eclipsed light and mystery enshrouded him. His voice grew deeper.

"There is more, there is always much, much more than what you hear—but not for this night. Tonight I am finished."

A wave of silence flooded the forests of Black Mountain. The creatures knew acts of courage. Bear's story had surely been one of them.

Coyote laughed, shattering the stillness.

"Excuse me, Shash, what about your old projecting teeth that overlap with phlegm strung like spiderwebs in your mouth? Have they a story too?"

There was no response, only red-green eyes flickering in the unnatural light of Shash's cave. Coyote's tail fell between his legs as he fled for the familiar sagebrush.

"Mountain Lion with dark yellow eyes, you nibble moon flowers. Have you a story to honor our parents this night?" And then Shash retreated.

Mountain Lion stepped forward, sleek and taut like a female bow.

"I have been present from the beginning. Though you may find surprise in what I am about to say, your instincts will nod with my cajoling tongue. I am one of your guardians with Black-god, Big Snake, Bear, and Deer Woman. (All of whom Mountain Lion spoke stepped forward and bowed.) We were the first Animal Chiefs. We were the leaders of the Hunter People. I hunt today from my home on tiptoes."

Deer Woman whispered to her young, "This is so. When Lion roars he takes the power away from us so that we become weak and cannot run very fast."

"I can carry one of you home. But remember this is so, only if you will it to be."

Deer Woman raised her head in accord. "And so it is."

"I hang back behind crimson cliffs and watch the light."

Mountain Lion stopped momentarily. "Have you seen the sky the color of wet juniper berries?"

She continued: "My life is now an elusive one. At dusk I am a feline amaranth. You imagine me and therefore I am. The soft pads on my feet are a weaver's gift, for I recognize the nap of napes instantly. At noon I am the color of sand. Perhaps you have seen my tail switching secrets with the Winds. My nose contemplates all of you."

Mountain Lion leaned forward and gave several quick chirps. "Just so you know. . ."

No doubt, this was an evening of disclosure. The animals checked to see if they were fully clothed, for at times the air seemed uncomfortably thin.

"Pay attention, my friends," said Shash. "Tonight where much is given, much is expected of us. Our skins of fur have been removed, only it is too dark for you to tell. We are wearing coats of trust. When one tells a story this is what happens."

The clouds seemed to swirl around Moon, which was now an overripened peach hanging in the eastern sky.

Badger crawled out of his den and abruptly spoke. "When the Sky and Earth made contact once before, not only did Coyote spring forth, but so did I."

Wild murmurings echoed in the canyons of Black Mountain.

"On a night very much like this one, I crawled back into the hole of our emergence, when in fact I am a child of the Sky."

Coyote, far removed from the gathering, could be heard bickering with the night.

"No one has ever doubted your power," said Black-god to Badger. "You are a steady, hard-working, intelligent creature. This comes as no message of astonishment."

"There are exceptions," reminded Blue and Yellow Fox coyly. "We cannot let Badger go without remembering the separation of sexes when he went among the women and made them wild with desire!"

"That is not to be forgotten," sneered Badger, "but neither are you two and Coyote! I was not alone in copulating with them and licking them between their legs."

Lightness entered the circle of beasts. Badger had passed them a candle of humor. They laughed at their complicity.

Skunk emerged. "I have tricked you before and thus cheated myself. Tonight under these amorous conditions, I want you to know Striped Skunk is female, and I, Spotted Skunk, am male. That is all."

Badger, who once participated with Striped Skunk in a series of four contests and lost, said, "We have known all along, but that you would finally come forth means a great deal."

A pause allowed for a period of privacy.

Deer Woman finally stood and said, "The antlers on my people's heads are feathers. This is why we can run through the woods silently."

Goshawk nodded. "We are relatives."

Next, Beaver waddled forward and sang: "Water is my business!" And all the Animals blessed him.

While the singing continued, Porcupine quietly walked behind the Animal People and thanked Black-god for letting him be his doorkeeper.

"That is your place, Old Buckskin. I knew you were more than A-messy-object-in-a-tree. When Monster Slayer was pursued by Tracking Bear, he was protected by the rattle of a slim-leaved yucca fruit held in his left hand and some twigs of hard oak in his right. He shot the monster, cut off its claws and large canine teeth, and took the gall and windpipe as trophies . . . the nipples became pinyon nuts, half of a piece of fat cut from around the tail ran off as a bear; the other half came toward him as a porcupine. These are your origins, Dahsání. Now go and feel proud that you, too, have a story to share."

"*Tso's, tso's, tso's!*" "Where is Chipmunk?" "Where is Chipmunk?" sang the Swallows. "We need to hear about the least of our clan being the bravest!" The Bluebirds ushered him in.

Haazeists'osi came forth and reverently turned so that all might see his fine striping.

"It went like this. . . ."

"Yes, tell us again and again," they all cheered.

"Monster Slayer was in the final slaying of Burrowing Monster."

"We remember him! We remember him!"

"Monster Slayer assumed Burrowing Monster was dead. . . ."

"Was he? Was he?"

"Just to make certain the noble deed was secured, I crawled out to the very end of Burrowing Monster's horn. . . ."

A stampede of hooves and paws and feathered feet went out in praise of Chipmunk.

"When I got to the point of Burrowing Monster's horn, I noticed that his woolly ears were still twitching! So I cried out, 'Tso's, Tso's, Tso's, Tso's!' meaning that Burrowing Monster was still alive."

"Let me finish the story," said Gopher, proud of his relative's accomplishments.

"Monster Slayer was indebted to Chipmunk's bravery, for he himself could have been caught and killed when the monster revived. As a reward, Monster Slayer allowed Chipmunk to streak his face and stripe his body with Burrowing Monster's blood!"

All agreed it was a very fine deed. After Chipmunk and Gopher had completed their story, Prairie Dog quietly entered the circle. She could not speak. Shash reminded her to breathe. Then she said, simply, "Should we ever be taken away from our village, there will be no one to cry for the rain. . . ." The Animal People knew exactly what Dlǫ́ǫ́ was saying.

The remainder of the evening was serendipitous. The Animal People danced in slow-moving circles covering vast areas of space. Clouds sifted stars as bats created pindrops of sound. Eyes were redirected toward Moon. It was over now. Moon's brilliance was restored and Sun and Earth had returned to their designated places in the Navajo universe. But life among the Animal People was different. Stories told from the heart had at once freed them and bound them more closely together. That happens you know, when stories are told well.

Black God flew through the last flames of the fire singing, "*Gwa, Gwa, Gwa, Gwa. . . .*"

Dawn was approaching and the voices of Hermit Thrush and Robin were growing restless. As the Animals began to scatter on Black Mountain, Begochidi stood tall, draped in dew, and exhorted, "Go now and be dressed in wind."

Shash was last to be seen walking slowly toward the top of Black Mountain.

I was there—I collected each story as it fell from the mouths of the Animals. Flea's strength would surprise you. At dawn the next day, I resumed my form and found my pouch of stories secure around my neck. I fastened it tightly so no tales could escape. I left my rabbit whistle at the base of Black Mountain. Home was in my gait.

I skirted the river's banks until I knew I had to cross. The currents had been following me for miles and I did not like their feel.

Once in the water I slipped, suffering seven somersaults over the homes of chubs and minnows. I begged them to help me, as I was so disoriented I knew I would never be able to find my way to land.

The next thing I remember is lying on a grey rock. I was dressed in silt. My pouch was gone. My stories gone. I was humiliated and I cried.

As my eyes cleared, I saw a lizard looking up at me with his head cocked in a lizard sort of way. The pouch of stories was a collar around his neck. This is what he said:

"Not far from here, not long from now, the only thing left of us will be that which is remembered. Not by choice, but by folly. The River Currents stole your pouch because they were afraid you would never open it, and then where would the Animal People be? What you heard last night under the eclipsed moon was not a requiem but a rejoicing."

It was almost noon, about the time Mountain Lion turns to sand.

"I will tell you this," Lizard continued. "Come out often —stroke my back, then tell your friends. We will live longer that way. Keep a story only long enough to give it away. Our future lies in our tales. . . ."

Then, in an instant, Hawk came down and grabbed Lizard's tail—and Lizard ran off to grow another.

9

DEERSKIN

I REMEMBER, AS A SMALL GIRL, WAKING UP ONE MORNING to the wild enthusiasm of my father and brothers. They were outside my bedroom window, and I could vaguely hear them talking about some sort of tracks they had found. Their voices conveyed a sense of awe as well as excitement. Not wanting to miss anything, I ran out to see.

The front door had been left open, and through it I could see all four of them crouching in the snow.

"Deer tracks . . ." my father said, touching them gently.

"Deer tracks," I said. "So?"

"Deer tracks," my brother restated emphatically.

"Deer tracks," I said again under my breath. No, something was missing when I said it. Feeling out of place and out of touch, I went back inside and shut the door. Through the glass I watched the passion that flowed between my father and brothers as they spoke of deer. Their words went beyond the occasion.

Many years have passed since that morning, but I often reflect on the relationship my brothers and father share with deer. Looking back and looking forward into the Navajo Way, I have come to realize the power of oral traditions, of stories, even in our own culture, and how they color our perceptions of the world around us.

Nowhere is this relationship of earth and story more poignant than in the Navajo perception of living things, *nanise*. The Diné have been told in their origin histories that they will receive knowledge from the Holy People, from plants and animals. As with other Indian peoples, the Navajo do not "rank-order" animals. Barry Lopez writes

> Each creature, from deer mouse to meadowlark, is respected for the qualities it best seems to epitomize; when those particular qualities are desired by someone, then that animal is approached as one who knows much about the subject. . . .

And elsewhere:

> In the native view, each creature carried information about the order of the universe—both at a practical level (ravens might reveal the presence of caribou to hunters), and at the level of augury. Moreover, each creature had its own special kind of power, and a person who wished knowledge in those areas—of patience, of endurance, of humor —would be attentive to those animals who possessed these skills.

Gregory Bateson points out in *Mind and Nature* that ". . . the very word, 'animal,' means endowed with mind and spirit."

This idea of animal mentors is illustrated in the Navajo Deerhunting Way. The Deerhunting Way is a blessing rite, a formula for corresponding with deer in the appropriate manner. Traditionally, hunters would participate in this ritual as a means to a successful hunt and their own personal safety.

Claus Chee Sonny, a Navajo medicine man who lives in the Tunitcha mountains near the Arizona-New Mexico border, tells the following story, which is part of the Deerhunting Way. He learned the Deerhunting Way from his father, who obtained it from his father, who was instructed by his father—Claus Chee's grandfather—and the many teachers who preceded him. The First People who taught the Deerhunting Way were the Deer Gods themselves. The Deer supplied the first divine hunters with the knowledge that was necessary to hunt them. And so the story begins:

> There was a hunter who waited in ambush. Wind had told him, "This is where the tracks are. The deer will come marching through in single file." The hunter had four arrows: one was made from sheet lightning, one of zigzag lightning, one of sunlight roots, and one of rainbow.
>
> Then the first deer, a large buck with many antlers, came. The hunter got ready to shoot the buck. His arrow was already in place. But just as he was ready to shoot, the deer transformed himself into a mountain mahogany bush, *tsé ésdaazii*. After a while, a mature man stood up from behind the bush. He stood up and said, "Do not shoot! We are your

neighbors. These are the things that will be in the future when human beings will have come into existence. This is the way you will eat us." And he told the hunter how to kill and eat the deer. So the hunter let the mature Deerman go for the price of his information. And the Deerman left.

Then the large doe, a shy doe, appeared behind the one who had left. The hunter was ready again to shoot the doe in the heart. But the doe turned into a cliffrose bush, *awééts'áál*. A while later a young woman stood up from the bush. The woman said, "Do not shoot! We are your neighbors. In the future, when man has been created, men will live because of us. Men will use us to live on." So then, for the price of her information, the hunter let the Doewoman go. And she left.

Then a young buck, a two-pointer, came along. And the hunter got ready to shoot. But the deer transformed himself into a dead tree, *tsin bisgá*. After a while, a young man stood up from behind the dead tree and said, "In the future, after man has been created, if you talk about us the wrong way we will cause trouble for you when you urinate, and we will trouble your eyes. We will also trouble your ears if we do not approve of what you say about us." And at the price of his information, the hunter let the young Deerman go.

Then the little fawn appeared. The hunter was ready to shoot the fawn, but she turned into a lichen-spotted rock, *tsé dláád*. After a while, a young girl stood up from the rock and spoke: "In the future all this will happen if we approve, and whatever we shall disapprove shall all be up to me. I am in charge of all the other Deer People. If you talk badly about us, and if we disapprove of what you say, I am the one who will respond with killing you. I will kill you with what I am. If you hear the cry of my voice, you will know that trouble is in store for you. If you do not make use of us properly, even in times when we are numerous, you will not see us anymore. We are the four deer who have transformed themselves into different kinds of things. Into these four kinds of things can we transform ourselves. Moreover, we can assume the form of all the different kinds of plants. Then when you look, you will not see us. In the future, only those of whom we approve shall eat the mighty deer. If, when you hunt, you come across four deer, you will not kill all of them. You may kill three and leave one. But if you kill all of us, it is not good.

"These are the things which will bring you happiness. When you kill a deer, you will lay him with the head toward your house. You will cover the earth with plants or with branches of trees lengthwise, with the growing tips of the plants pointing the direction of the deer's head, toward your house. So it shall be made into a thick padding, and the deer shall be laid on that. Then you will take us home to your house and eat of us. You will place our bones under any of the things whose form we can assume—mountain mahogany, cliffrose, dead tree, lichen-spotted rock, spruce, pine, or under any of the other good plants. At these places you may put our bones. You will sprinkle the place with yellow pollen. Once. Twice. Then you lay the bones. And then you sprinkle yellow pollen on top of the bones. This is for the protection of the game animals. In this manner they will live on; their bones can live again and live a lasting life."

This is what the little fawn told the hunter. "You

will be able to use the entire body of the deer, even
the skin. And we belong to Talking-god. We belong
to Black-god. We are in his hands. And he is able to
make us deaf and blind. Those among you, of
whom he approves, are the good people. They will
hunt with success and will be able to kill us. According to his own decisions he will surrender us
to the people. The Black-god is Crow. But when
you hunt you do not refer to him as Crow but as
Black-god."

Then, referring to what the fawn had said, the
other three deer said, "This is what will be. And
this is what will be. And this is how it is."

So these are the four who gave information; the large
buck, the doe, the two-pointer, and the fawn. Man was
created later. All these events happened among the Gods,
prior to the creation of man. All animals were like human
beings then; they were able to speak. Thus, this story was
not made up by old Navajo men. These events were
brought about by Black-god. Then, after having obtained
all this information, the hunter let the four deer go.

As final hunting instructions, Claus Chee Sonny shares
the Deer People's knowledge:

You will not throw the bones away just anywhere.
Everything of which we are made, such as our skin,
meat, bones, is to be used. . . . Anything that we
hold onto, such as the earth from the four sacred
mountains, the rainbow, the jewels, the corn, all
the plants we eat, will be in us. Our bodies contain
all these. And because of this we are very useful. . . .
Needles can be made from the bones of the front
and hind legs. This is what we use to stitch buck-

skin together. . . . A deer not killed by a weapon shall be used in the sacred ceremonies. All the meat is very useful. You can put deer meat as medicine on sheep, on horses, and on other domestic animals. All livestock lives because of deer.

The usefulness of the deer is the foundation which has been laid. It serves as an example for other things. This is what is meant when we say that the deer are first in all things.

Through the Deerhunting Way one can see many connections, many circles. It becomes a model for ecological thought expressed through mythological language. The cyclic nature of the four deers' advice to the hunter is, in fact, good ecological sense. Out of the earth spring forth plants on which the animals feed. The animal, in time, surrenders its life so that another may live, and as its body parts are returned to earth, new life will emerge and be strengthened once again. Do not be greedy. Do not be wasteful. Remember gratitude and humility for all forms of life. Because they are here, we are here. They are the posterity of Earth.

It is this kind of oral tradition that gives the Navajo a balanced structure to live in. It provides continuity between the past and the future. They know how to behave. Stories channel energy into a form that can heal as well as instruct. This kind of cosmology enables a person to do what is appropriate and respect the rights of others. N. Scott Momaday tells the following story:

There was a man living in a remote place on the Navajo reservation who had lost his job and was having a difficult time making ends meet. He had a wife and several children. As a matter of fact, his

wife was expecting another child. One day a friend
came to visit him and perceived that his situation
was bad. The friend said to him, "Look, I see you
are in tight straits. I see you have many mouths to
feed, and that you have no wood and that there is
very little food in your larder. But one thing puz-
zles me. I know you are a hunter, and I know, too,
there are deer in the mountains very close at hand.
Tell me, why don't you kill a deer so that you and
your family might have fresh meat to eat?" And
after a time the man replied, "No, it is inappropriate
that I should take life just now when I am expecting the gift of life."

True freedom is having *no* choice. In this case, the man
knew exactly what he had to do with respect to the land.
Behavior became gesture. "It isn't a matter of intellection.
It is respect for the understanding of one's heritage. It is
a kind of racial memory, and it has its origin beyond any
sort of historical experience. It reaches back to the dawn of
time."

My thoughts return to that winter morning—to the deer
tracks—and then to a crisp day in October when finally, at
the age of sixteen, my father invited me to go deer hunting
with him in the Dolores Triangle of Colorado. We participated in the rituals associated with the season, clothing
ourselves in yellow sweatshirts, fluorescent orange vests,
and red caps. We polished our boots with mink oil and
rubbed Cutter's insect repellent all over our bodies, so as
not to be bothered by remaining insects. We rose before
the sun, and stalked west ridges to catch the last of day's
light. Finally, around the campfire, I listened to the stories
my father told until the stars had changed positions many
times.

It was only then that I realized a small fraction of what my father knew, of what my brothers knew about deer. My brothers had been nurtured on such tales, and for the first time I saw the context they had been told in. My education was limited because I had missed years, layers of stories.

Walk lightly, walk slowly,
look straight ahead
with the corners of your eyes open.
Stay alert, be swift.
Hunt wisely
in the manner of deer.

I walked with reverence behind my father, trying to see what he saw. All at once he stopped, put his index finger to his mouth, and motioned me to come ahead. Kneeling down among the scrub oak, he carefully brushed aside some fallen leaves. "Deer tracks," he said.

"Deer tracks," I whispered.

10

WOOL

PICTURE A BRONZED WOMAN TENDING HER FLOCK OF SHEEP. She is dressed in lavender and turquoise, akin to earth and sky. She moves slowly across the vermillion sand as her skirt sweeps sage. Occasionally she looks upward, her scarf flowing in the breeze, but her steady pace brings her look forward as she sends her sheep west. The spirit of Changing Woman encircles her deeply etched face; she is erasing years of living.

Imagine an adopted Anglo son wanting to share the civilized world with his Navajo father who, in ninety years or so, had never seen a paved road or a train. Barre Toelken tells of this experience when he showed his father a two-page spread of the Empire State Building. As he expounded on the building's remarkable qualities, his father interrupted to ask, "How many sheep will it hold?"

Inside the Cultural Center in Shiprock, twelve women weave, spin, and card. Wool. The wool is the fleece from their sheep. As they wash, comb, pull, and weave, sheep are running through their fingers.

> Spider Woman instructed the Navajo women how to weave on a loom which Spider Man told them how to make. The crosspoles were made of sky and earth cords, the warp sticks of sun rays, the healds of rock crystal and sheet lightning. The batten was a sun halo; white shell made the comb. There were four spindles: one a stick of zigzag lightning with a whorl of cannel coal; one a stick of flash light-ning with a whorl of turquoise; a third had a stick of sheet lightning with a whorl of abalone; a rain streamer formed the stick of the fourth, and its whorl was white shell.

. . . and then, sheep ran through the warp.

To the Navajo, *dibé*, sheep, are more than sheer eco-nomics. They are a way of life.

> Sheep and goats, which had been brought into the Southwest by the Spaniards, provided a larger and

more dependable food supply, and this was a fundamental condition of Navaho population increase. Furthermore, livestock animals, wool and mohair, hides, and woolen textiles revolutionized Navaho economy in another way: They supplied a steady source of salable or exchangeable wealth, permitting the acquisition of metal tools and manufactured articles.

And so the Navajo stand today.

Whenever I take this piece of fleece out of my bag, the children immediately giggle and smile; it is as though wool unleashes in them all the playfulness associated with sheep —not sheep in isolation, but home. Not too long ago young children spent the bulk of their childhood herding. Although today school fills the time once reserved for sheep, it is not uncommon for some children to miss days of school on account of tending responsibilities.

In Navajoland, sheep are the link between the old and the young.

Extended families—aunts, uncles, cousins, and grandparents—all participate in the herding of sheep. Gladys Reichard describes a "sheep dip sing" that she attended in the early 1930s:

At the sheep dip all is action. A number of saddled horses tethered to a small piñon stand in a circle. At a short distance a shade has been erected. From one of its posts hangs a sheep, just slaughtered, which a woman vigorously skins. Not far from her feet another woman sitting on the ground is cleaning the intestines. Farther away a woman and a young girl are tending a small cedar fire from which rise wisps of white smoke like the gentlest of clouds thrown off the towcards of the Wind Gods. Near the sharp edge of the wash a girl, shawl over head, stands before a resting flock that is awaiting its turn at the chute.

A smell of live sheep mixes with the odor of cedar smoke as we advance into the thick of the activities. Several hundred bleating, baaing sheep, wondering and frightened, mill about in the corral from which a narrow chute leads to the dipping trough. Men and boys stand thick on the sides of the chute with prods in their hands, urging the reluctant animals toward the jumping-off platform. . . . One after another the balking creatures slip, jump, or are pushed into the trough with a splash that speckles all within its radius. They are dipped for prevention and curing of scabies. Close along both sides of the long narrow trough stand Navajo women, young and old, and young men—all with long forked sticks. They see to it that the animals are thoroughly doused. . . . It is the hardest kind of work.

So often we compare the economics of traditional cultures with our own, without taking into consideration the intangibles. Personal connections. Ritual.

Early in the morning we take the sheep out of the corral. I sing a song and open the gate. When the sheep are half out my song is half finished. When they are all out I stop my song.

Such was the case when the United States government initiated its sheep reduction program. This is a striking example of a dominant culture's insensitivity and ignorance toward Native People's ways.

In 1868, after the Long Walk period, the Navajo had few sheep left. The government issued approximately 14,000 sheep to The People in small family lots. Perhaps more. The philosophy of the administration at the time was quantity expansion and exploitation of nature. The Navajo were encouraged to increase their flocks. That is exactly what happened. Within a few years their livestock had outgrown the land's capacity to feed them and still maintain its plant cover. The 1899 report of the commissioner of Indian Affairs said that the tribe owned 1,000,000 sheep, 250,000 goats, and more than 100,000 horses. Fragile, dry rangeland could not support such large flocks and herds for long. As the range became severely overgrazed, the rainwater previously absorbed by ground cover pelted the soil until deep gullies were cut. Erosion.

By 1933 the erosion problem had become so serious that the government, under a different administration, devised the sheep reduction program. If the number of animals on the range were reduced, the same amount of feed could produce higher quality sheep, and thus raise income. When the facts were laid out on the table in Washington, it made perfect sense. Very rational. But the Navajo did not see it that way. To them, large herds of sheep were not just sources of meat to be marketed but symbols of prestige and honorable living. But the program was enacted.

When we tamper with the balance of things the scales rarely meet equilibrium again. This story is written over and over in our history, be it with Native Peoples, economics, or bears. We are grossly insensitive to the connectedness of life. Eric Hoffer makes the point: "Lack of sensitivity is basically an unawareness of ourselves." In terms of culture which is intrinsically linked with landscape, is it possible to meet another with empathetic eyes? Perhaps. If we can begin to focus beyond ourselves.

When a Navajo looks at a building and says, "How many sheep will it hold?" he is saying, "What value does this have in my life?"

I left on the 7:00 P.M. Trailways bus for Monticello, Utah. I was nervous. You know all those horror stories associated with bus terminals, especially in western boomtowns, of which there were many en route. I'll just keep to myself, I thought, sit behind the driver with my healthy supply of pumpkin bread. We pulled out of Salt Lake City on a November night.

We hadn't been gone a minute when I discovered two young Navajo boys sitting behind me.

"Yá'át'ééh," I said, smiling.

They huddled together and giggled.

"Hello," they answered in unison.

"Are you guys scared?"

Their hands were hiding their mouths. They nodded their heads.

"Me too."

I had a couple of skulls in my satchel. Good conversation pieces.

"What do you suppose these are?" I asked casually.

They looked up in disbelief and began giggling again. The elder brother subtly shoved his elbow into the younger one's side. They became deadly serious.

"We don't know."

"Excuse me," I said, "I can't hear you."

The younger brother leaned forward. "My brother said we don't know."

"Do you want to look at them?"

"Yes, please."

Five or so minutes went by and I could hear animated dialogue behind me, all in Navajo, so I didn't understand what was being said. I rearranged myself and slid further into my seat, leaning against the window. I could feel sleep coming on.

All of a sudden, from the corner of my eye, I could see a dark little hand holding a white skull, waving in the air. I looked up and two faces hung down.

"This one's a deer and this one's a mountain lion."

"Oh, really?" I said. "How so?"

"We know them. They live by us and we've seen them."

We exchanged names and told each other where we were from and where we were going. It happened that Hoskie Nakai and his older brother, Darold, were on the Indian placement program of the Mormon church. They were living with a foster family in Idaho, and returning to Cuba City, New Mexico, for Thanksgiving. We kept each other company.

I remember that evening vividly. We were approaching Soldier Summit and huge clusters of snowflakes flew at the big windshield. I felt as though we were traveling in space with billions of stars coming at us in the black void.

I used to think I had to ask children about nature in order to talk about nature. But on this particular night I learned you begin with sheep. Because people were trying to sleep on the bus, Hoskie, Darold, and I exchanged notes back and forth, long notes. . . .

"So, you're going home?"

"Yes, New Mexico is the most beautiful country. They have everything, even red sand."

"What do you do when you're home?"

"Herd sheep."

"What's that like?"

"It's a lot of fun. You get to know the sheep, the flowers, and the animals around you. You think about them and the grass they eat. Sometimes we play and sometimes we kill lizards and hunt rabbits."

"How do you herd sheep?"

"When you are herding sheep on a horse you let them out of the corral and let them eat and eat and eat, as much as they want. Later on, at around two or three o'clock in the afternoon, you are supposed to herd the sheep back to the house. A sheep looks like a dog, but it has a lot of wool and they don't bark. They say, 'Baa, baa.' "

Hoskie leaned over the seat. "Can I tell you why I like it?" He then continued to write: "I like to herd sheep a lot because I get to know all about them. I get a lot of money from the wool and meat that comes from the sheep. Two things you have to know: how to butcher a sheep and how to cut the wool and make it into a rug. You usually get a lot of money from rugs. But the thing I like best about herding sheep is that you get to learn about the grass the sheep eat."

"Who teaches you how to herd sheep?" I wrote back in shaky handwriting, as the bus was changing gears.

"My grandpa. Grandfathers teach their grandsons. My grandpa told me to guard the sheep very carefully, so the coyote won't eat one of them and he told me to let the sheep eat a lot of grass, as much as they want. My grandpa told me not to rush the sheep when they drink water. He said we have all the time in the world."

"What else do your grandparents teach you?"

"My grandmother taught us how to butcher a sheep. First, you cut the head off, then you skin the body. After that you take out all the guts and then put them in a pan and save them until you are hungry."

He passed the notepad forward and then said, "Wait, I forgot something."

"They also tell us stories about the old days, about Coyote and Crow."

My turn again. "Have you ever seen a coyote while you were out with the sheep?"

"Once, my cousin and I were herding sheep back to the corral and we saw a coyote. It saw the sheep and he was going to get one because he was hungry. We were scared. We didn't know what to do. Then we had a plan. We threw some rocks at the coyote. He ran down the hill."

Darold and Hoskie were laughing. They slipped me another note on the back of their bus pass.

"P.S. What do you do when you're home?"

By this time all three of us were in the same seat. I told them I liked to watch birds. I told them one day I closed my eyes and visited a very special place called Black-tail Pond.

"I was sitting on an old cottonwood log with my feet outstretched. I could roll back and forth at my leisure. There seemed to be edges all around me: the edge of the river, the edge of the meadow, and the edge of the cottonwood grove. The air was like cold steel. Clouds were the color of salmon, swimming west with the sun as it sank behind tall, jagged peaks. Blue. Lavender shadows were growing longer and longer. I could still hear birdsong and a few mergansers were taking flight, leaving the river for night roosting. A doe and two fawns crossed the meadow and entered the interface of trees. Dusk. As I turned around—a grey owl stood, silver-tipped and full. Grey Owl handed me a golden feather and spoke to me in words I do not remember. I only felt the embrace of owl fur. I was weak and I shivered. Grey Owl lifted me to many, many places. We explored untold terrain.

"When I opened my eyes, I was looking into the eyes of my silver-tipped Grandmother. She was wearing a golden feather on her breast. Grey Owl."

Silence filled us and I appreciated the moment the boys gave me. But it was short-lived.

"Is that true?" they asked.

"Yes," I said. "It's all true."

"We thought so. . . ."

The bus rolled along through sagebrush flats. It had stopped snowing. We were further south now. Tiny colored lights bordered the horizon like glass beads, a hint of civilization. Hoskie sat up.

"Terry, the real reason we are coming home is because our grandmother died. . . ."

I looked into their faces but could not speak. We held each other. All I could sense was loss—theirs, mine, all of ours.

"My grandmother was a weaver. She knew many designs that no one knew but her children. She told me that weaving wasn't hard so I tried my best and now I know how to weave better than I thought I could. She told me I could weave good, so now I know!"

Darold had retreated into his own thoughts. Hoskie went on talking.

"Sometimes, I see designs when I herd sheep and sometimes I don't. My grandmother told me it's a good time to look for designs when you're with the sheep because it is their wool that you weave with. You just look at things like flowers or clouds. They give you lots of designs. They're all out there by the sheep."

A pause followed.

"But sometimes, when I am lying on my back and I look over and my foster brother is asleep, I look up at the ceiling and see my grandmother's designs. My grandmother's designs come back to me and I feel her walking in the room. I feel as though she is holding me. . . ."

Once again, a pause traveled with us. We slept periodically, ate pieces of pumpkin bread, but talked very little after that. No need.

The bus pulled into Monticello right on schedule, 3:25 A.M. My body and eyes ached, reminders that the sooner I could find a long bed to lie in the better off I'd be. The bus doors folded open. A wave of cold air rushed in. As I got up to leave, I looked at Hoskie and Darold, who were curled around each other, asleep. I leaned over and kissed them.

"Remember your grandparents," I whispered.

"Remember yours too," they whispered back.

I thought they were sleeping. I was wrong. We said our goodbyes and I promised to send them some plastic dinosaurs from the museum. The bus left, a little behind schedule, and drove on through Cuba, New Mexico.

11

A
POTSHARD
AND
SOME CORN POLLEN

SILENCE. THAT IS TIME YOU ARE HEARING. WE ARE IN Anasazi country. This is a place where canyon walls rise upward like praying hands. Veins of water run between them. You may choose to walk here, ankle deep in the midst of chubs and minnows. If you wish you can brace your hands flush against either side of the slickrock and fancy yourself pushing down walls. Look up. The sky is a blue ribbon. These are the canyons, cool refuges from exposed heat, dripping with red mimulus and ferns. This is the landscape that gave these people birth.

To the Navajo, Anasazi means the Ancient Ones. In prehistoric days they inhabited the four-corners region, where Utah, Colorado, New Mexico, and Arizona share a common boundary point. There was a day in mid-November when the children of Montezuma Creek, Utah, took me by the hand and told me stories of Anasazi.

"Who are the Anasazi?" I asked as we were walking down to the river.

"They are the long-time-ago people who lived on this land. They are the relatives of the Hopi and Pueblo people. We find their baskets, sandals, and pottery but do not take them."

"Why not?"

"People say that if you take away their property and put it in your house a spirit will come and it will get you. It might even kill you. I don't know if it's true, but my grandmother told it to my sister and she threw away the pottery she had. That's why I don't take pottery. They also say that the long-time-ago people's spirit stays with their body and if you touch their bones you will have nightmares."

"Have you ever found any Anasazi bones?"

"Yes." We came to the river and sat down.

"You can find their houses around here, but we don't go in. I know where some ruins are by my aunt and uncle's place. And up from Calf Creek Wash there are one hundred and sixty-three white handprints slapped on the red face of the rock. [Anasazi applause, I thought, as gooseflesh appeared on my skin.] And then below that the rocks have waves in them and everywhere you look you can find Anasazi rocks."

"What do you mean?"

"Anasazi rocks—these . . ." I looked down to where little fingers pointed, and sure enough the children had located countless pieces of pottery, all of which I had mistaken for sandstone or shale.

You cannot travel very long through Navajoland without stubbing your toe on the Anasazi. You can feel these things the children speak of, for the wind carries voices: Every conversation, every sigh uttered by the "long-time-ago people" circulates above you. Perhaps that's why the clouds move so quickly in the Southwest.

Cerulean skies and deep vinaceous bands of sandstone become places of power. Pit houses dug in the earth and cliff dwellings hanging on ledges still house the Anasazi spirit. Listen. You may hear music inside their ancient earth architecture. I have—I think.

There have been occasions when I stood in their ruins and found tiny shriveled cobs of corn, reminders that the genius of Anasazi lay in their ability to conserve and utilize scarce water and fertile soil, creating a farm-based culture in an area unsuited for such a subsistence pattern. Crops such as maize, beans, and squash were central to their survival.

And there is their pottery: black on white and black on red. You walk through sagebrush, down arroyos, and up hillsides innocently, until an irregular rock attracts your eye. You pick it up, turn it over, and realize this is pottery. I have held in my hands pieces of coiled pots . . . once wet clay rolled into a snake, then spiraled into a vessel. I have seen Anasazi fingerprints thousands of years old pinched into this clay to ensure tightness. Whole generations pass before you as you examine this ancient, domestic chip. Who made this? What did it belong to? How long has it been here? Like an onion, layers upon layers of civilization are peeled until, finally, you face the Anasazi bare.

Now you are caught in dilemma's web: What to do with this remnant of Anasazi life? Do you keep it? Take it home and place it on your mantel as a tangible reminder of your affinity with Desert People? ("Of course no one would appreciate it as I do.") Or do you turn this piece of clay in? Confess your findings to a local museum or nearby National Park Visitor's Center, trusting that they will find an appropriate home for it (most likely in drawer 240-B, after you have filled out USGS Form #A876-5 with your #2 lead pencil)? Or do you leave it ("But someone else will just come along and take it.") in the keeping of another thousand years to be kneaded back into desert sands?

PUBLIC—No. 209

An Act for the Preservation of American Antiquities

Be it enacted by the Senate and House of Representatives of the United States of America in Congress assembled, that any person who shall appropriate, excavate, injure, or destroy any historic or prehistoric ruin or monument, or any subject of antiquity, situated on lands owned or controlled by the Government of the United States without the permission of the Secretary of the Department of the Government having jurisdiction over the lands on which said antiquities are situated, shall upon conviction, be fined in a sum of not more than five hundred dollars or be imprisoned for a period of not more than ninety days, or shall suffer both fine and imprisonment, in the discretion of the court. . . . (Section 1)

Approved June 8, 1906 (34 Stat. L. 225)

We infer about another culture through their physical remains. The questions encircling ancient peoples' social systems could never even have been asked a few decades ago. Now we can speculate. Pottery patterns, designs, and motifs are providing clues as to whether the Anasazi were a matrilocal or a patrilocal society. If archaeologists find a continuum among pottery designs they can infer matrilineal order, with mother passing pottery motifs on to daughter as she brings her husband into the village. A hodgepodge of pottery designs suggests a patrilineal society, each man bringing in a woman with her individual design.

Stories. More stories. If these artifacts are lifted from their birthplace they cease to speak. Like a piece of coral broken from its reef, they lose their color, becoming pale and brittle. Somehow we need to acquaint ourselves with the art of letting go, for to own a piece of the past is to destroy it.

But it's a difficult thing to do. I know because I have pocketed a piece of pottery. In the context of all the desert's loveliness it became numinous. I had to possess it. Somewhere deep inside me I hoped this potshard might become a talisman, an amulet. I was wrong. What once glistened in those pastel sands collected dust on my dressing table. Its loss of dignity haunted me.

Lessons painfully learned evoke humility. I could never take a potshard now. Like Coyote's fur, I am wary of its power. It belongs to the earth and a culture which has passed through it. I remember holding a plaited Anasazi slipper, small, wide, and curled. As I carefully turned it over and over I kept thinking, "What is of value here—the sandal or the sandaled foot?"

AND NOW THE WALLS ARE WORN TO SAND,
AND LIE
LOW-RIDGED BENEATH THE VULTURE'S
LONELY FLIGHT.
—*"Seventh City of Cibola"*
HENRY NOYES PRATT

Chaco Canyon. The standing ruins have metamorphosed into standing rocks. From the sun-scorched earth they were taken, to the same soil they return. The cool breezes which run through them are the voice and spirit of Anasazi.

I have found these ruins to be as alive as I allow them to be. Sitting near the threshold of Pueblo Bonito, I rebuild these eroded walls with my imagination. Uneven skylines are immediately transformed into smooth, symmetrical pueblos. Remnants of this ancient village become a cornerstone to a thriving community. In the courtyard I see women dressed in crude tunics of hand-woven muslin. Some are grinding corn with their *manos* and *metates*; some are sitting on fibrous mats weaving baskets; others are pinching clay pots, already coiled; and a few women are retrieving water, carrying pots on their heads. I hear the laughter of children. They run in and out of hidden corridors, a terra-cotta maze. Domesticated turkeys squabble about. I listen to the mumbling of elders as they speak to one another. They lean against white adobe walls. I feel the power of holy men as they meet in giant *kivas* below. Corn pollen offerings are left in key-shaped doorways, the same corn pollen that can absorb a deer's spirit or bless a child. For this brief moment, the boundaries of time and space dissolve. Anasazi drums return.

Before leaving Chaco, I step inside a small pueblo room. I don't think anyone saw me; for some reason this is important. Solitude. Whitewashed walls. Hand prints, streaked across the surface. Female energy. I hold my hand against hers. Cold contact. Her hand, so much smaller, more square. I shiver. I picture a young woman sitting in the corner, legs outstretched—perhaps a babe at her breast. Silence. I don't want there to be: Silence. I want to talk, listen, share, spend entire afternoons in womanly conversation about her life, mine. Somehow, I sense that a thousand years do not separate us.

12

THE
STORYTELLER

THE CLAY FIGURINE THAT FALLS OUT OF MY POUCH IS A sacred tradition. The Storyteller. I found her in Jemez, New Mexico. When I saw her I knew I had met her before. Her body was rounded like earth. Stories. Breath. I have heard them before, again and again. I can hear them today, again and again—from my greatgrandmother, my grandmother, my mother—my storytellers. The children hanging on her back, climbing up her knees, resting in her lap are my brothers and sisters, cousins, me. Her eyes have been painted closed. I understand. To tell a story you must travel inward.

We have all been nurtured on stories. Story is the umbilical cord that connects us to the past, present, and future. Family. Story is a relationship between the teller and the listener, a responsibility. After the listening you become accountable for the sacred knowledge that has been shared. Shared knowledge equals power. Energy. Strength. Story is an affirmation of our ties to one another.

I have become acutely aware of story's circular logic as I've traveled among the Navajo. Coming from a tradition of inquiry, questions came out of my mouth much in the same way Snake's tongue probes for environmental clues. I was searching. I wanted to learn where I was and with whom. But the Navajos did not disclose themselves directly. They spoke to me through stories, obliquely obliging an inquisitive child. If you cared enough to stay awhile, to let go of immediacy, allowing your mind to drift in and out, a story was spun.

I remember asking a young boy, "What is the most important thing you learn in school?" I was expecting the usual linear response: "Reading, math, P.E." This was not the case. Instead, he shared the following story:

> I knew a boy who everyone thought was retarded. He was slow and had little life in him. He went to the BIA school away from home. Finally they sent him back to his family and told them he was of no use. The family transferred him to the Shiprock Alternative School, where he learned who he was. He was brought up by his cultural roots and felt support by his Navajo brothers and sisters. This boy became president of the student council.

What is the most important thing one learns in school? Self-esteem, support, and friendship, all poignantly revealed through story. As a result of many encounters such as this, the Navajo taught me to listen in a way I had never imagined.

Do I see this clay Storyteller's belly rise? Could it be she is making a motion to speak? I lean forward and recall Cecilia Etcitty of Rough Rock, Arizona. We met at Rough Rock Demonstration School where she taught kindergarten. I remember her hair to be dark and full, her eyes like pools of deep water. When she spoke her hands outlined images.

She told us she knew where all the colors of sand lived. She told the truth. In a very small radius, a rainbow had been grounded. There on a remote hillside were dozens of desert shades.

Celia invited us to make "sandscapes." She handed me a clear glass bottle. I tried to scrape off the last bit of labeling from its surface. I watched her filter the grains through her fingers. She was recreating the land where she lived. I left her and began on my own.

First I found a place accessible to as many colors as possible. I felt like the hands circling on a clock. The next step was simply a matter of choice: which sands? Carefully, I sifted colored bands into my bottle; white, mauve, lavender, rose, ochre, rust, olive-green, grey, periwinkle blue, mustard, beige, taupe. With a quick turn of my wrist, mesas appeared.

We spent the afternoon together. I felt as though we were sitting on a very old blanket as she wove me into one story after another. She spoke of sheep herding as a young girl, of running zigzag through the sage, and of open sky.

"I remember when I thought our home was around Black Mesa, underneath two clouds. They always seemed to be there. Guardians."

She told stories of *Kinaaldá*, and of the careful way her mother and aunts combed her black hair with the traditional mountain-grass brush in preparation for, in honor of her womanhood. I asked her about Changing Woman. She lowered her head saying, "This is not the time." Her voice became strong as she told of her 108-year-old grandmother who was born at Fort Sumner and made the Long Walk back to Rough Rock as a child.

"You see, this is my home. My traditions are planted here." She spoke of her grandmother's advice to follow the quiet life, and shared her fears of the time when her parents and grandparents will die.

"I'm afraid I will not know The Way."

We are not so different.

We watched the sun move across the sky and commented on the changing shadows—how they grew longer as the day progressed. She told me how important it is for the Navajo to rise and be counted.

> Sun is our father. He knows each one of us and when the first light shines upon the earth, He is making a count of His children. If you are awake and standing, you are counted as being alive. But if Sun peers inside your hogan and finds you lying down, asleep, you are counted as being dead.

"So, get up before that Sun and be counted as alive!" she said joyfully.

I couldn't help but laugh as I thought of all the years I have been counted as dead. I assured her that I would make my best effort to greet the dawn, even if it were from my mind's eye while I was dreaming.

Celia's face was the color of the deep amber soil she was

sitting on. I looked pale as I walked alongside her. Brown eyes, blue eyes; earth and ocean. As we parted, close to twilight, she handed me a bouquet of Navajo tea and some sprigs of juniper.

"Boil these tonight until they release their fragrance. Their juices will calm you."

I drank them, and they did.

The Storyteller pauses, breathes in deeply, and goes on. . . .

Rosa Benally, born of winter snow, is another storyteller, wise beyond her seventeen years. She breathes contemporary tradition, having been raised by her grandparents and schooled in Shiprock. Rosa is the new Navajo generation, with Dostoyevski in one hand and corn pollen in the other.

She tells of days when her grandfather rode on the backs of grizzly bears and lured rattlesnakes out of their dens by the power of a single word. I watched her eyes shift inward and sensed the Word passing through her heart. Silence. A prayer. She believes that ritual language is a part of her daily communion with the land, language that not only describes where she lives, but creates it. She sings:

> *The wild beasts, birds*
> *are my friends—*
> *Messengers.*
> *Protectors.*
> *Their sacred names,*
> *their ancient songs,*
> *are the keys to their world—*

a world of no time,
a world of harmony.
If everyone would look
to their beast and fowl brother,
one could learn
the mysteries of Mother Earth.
They were created by the Great One
to aid us five fingers. To
aid us in our need for food,
to be our teachers
in the lessons Mother Earth has for us.
And our Mother, the Earth,
the beautiful woman
whom we live on,
the trails of life that she adorns
are the trails we travel.
In my path,
my life,
I shall always look to nature
because I am a child of nature
in spirit.

Before dawn of the next day, Rosa and I slip into the male waters of the San Juan River. We immerse ourselves in clay-colored water; I look upward and see Venus in the western sky, sparkling. Rosa's eyes reflect new moon. We wash each other's bodies with sage and dance obeisantly around the gentle rapids—arms outstretched, waists turning, breasts loose. Refreshed and renewed, we emerge onto the river's banks. We sink our toes into the cold sand and bow our heads. Shiver. In silence we lift the sun.

Storytelling awakens us to that which is real. Honest. It is the most pure form of communication because it transcends the individual. The Kalahari Bushmen have said, "A story is like the wind. It comes from a far-off place, and we feel it." Those things that are most personal are most general, and are, in turn, most trusted. Stories bind. They are connective tissues. They are basic to who we are.

A story has a composite personality which grows out of its community. It maintains a stability within that community, providing common knowledge as to how things are, how things should be—knowledge based in experience. These stories become the conscience of the group. They belong to everyone.

But what about earth and story? Simon Ortiz, the Pueblo poet, says, "In continuance of the stories and songs —the earth shall continue." Oral tradition reminds one of community and community in the Native American sense encompasses all life-forms: people, land, and creatures. Barry Lopez extends this notion when he says, "The correspondence between the interior landscape and exterior landscape is story."

Landscape shapes culture. Aldo Leopold states, "The rich diversity of the world's cultures reflects a corresponding diversity in the wilds that gave them birth." Perhaps we can begin to find the origins of our cultural inheritance in the land—not to move backwards, but forward to understanding the profound interconnectedness of all living things. As Gregory Bateson says, "If the world be connected . . . then thinking in terms of stories must be shared by all mind or minds, whether ours or those of redwood forests and sea anemones."

I remember meeting Herb Blatchford, a Navajo holyman, in Albuquerque, New Mexico. I asked him if it were appropriate for a non-Indian to use Indian stories to illustrate a land ethic.

He looked directly into my eyes. "That is why they were created." I tried not to waver.

"Does it offend you?" I asked.

"No, it does not offend me. But it may some. But some have a deeper knowledge than others."

It is true that native stories rooted in landscape evoke a sense of integrity, of wonder toward the earth and all its creatures. Animals are given "mythic proportion," to clarify certain values, attitudes, and lessons. In contrast, animals are not mystified in Anglo tradition. The wolf is stereotyped by "Little Red Riding-Hood" and "The Three Little Pigs." Is this inherent to wolfness?

We are not Navajo, however; we are not Inuit people or Sioux. We are contemporary citizens living in a technological world. Swimming in crosscultural waters can be dangerous, and if you are honest you can't stay there very long. Sooner or later you have to look at your own reflection and decide what to do with yourself.

We are urban people. We make periodic pilgrimages to the country. Each of us bears a unique relationship with landscape if we allow ourselves to let go—let go of cultural biases and societal constraints, taking the time to experience earth as it is, raw and self-defined. We need to imagine ourselves flying on the backs of owls, for a people without natural vision is a people without insight. We have the power to rethink our existence, our time in earth's embrace, and step forward with compassionate intelligence. If we align ourselves with the spirit of place we will find humility infused with joy.

The land holds stories. We can learn the stories natural history has to teach and marvel as a child over its simple design. We can begin walking, trusting our own experiences and thinking about all the imagination can bring. It is here that a small bird can land on a Christmas tree with a fire burning. It disappears and we are left holding a feather.

These are the stories that come to us and sing the mysteries which surround us. Oral tradition is always one step from being lost. And now much of the earth walks alongside. A story keeps things known—and in the case of the natural world, few are literate. Have we felt the movements of snakes or experienced a happy tongue among huckleberries? Do we know the songs of native grasses or the prayers of migrating birds? We can confront the mysteries of life directly by involving ourselves, patiently and quietly, in the day-to-day dramas of the land. To ask a question and find a story about an episode of earth is to remember who we are. Wild rivers run through our veins.

One need not live in the wilderness to bear the rights of a spirited storyteller. An urban naturalist can transform city lights into stars because he or she knows the difference.

Through the Navajo culture, I have come back to my own. I can travel to Navajo Mountain for "Pioneer Days" and watch women cook mutton stew over the fire while foot races are being run. Or I can attend "The Days of '47 Parade," in Salt Lake City, and watch my great-aunts slice watermelons as floats pass by.

The little Jemez Storyteller who sits on my desk breathes in and out, in and out, and gradually I see myself. Navajo rugs become handmade quilts, pieces of the old creating something new.

My leather pouch has served me well carrying stories from the desert; a sprig of sage; rocks, sand, and seed; a bouquet of feathers bound by yarn; coyote fur and a bone from Black Mountain; deerskin; wool; a potshard and some corn pollen. When I had no tales to tell, they drew me to The People. Now I can give them away.

Harold Drake said this, after his family had just finished putting on another Pioneer Day celebration at the base of Navajo Mountain:

"I am the land. You are the land. The Great Spirit creates all this—man, woman, the mountain, the rain that takes care of everything. You have to respect yourself first. Begin here."

I have work to do. A group of children is waiting downstairs for a museum tour. Perhaps we will sit in a circle and pass around an ancient basket and tell stories of a past people, or maybe we will go outside and find our own.

13

HOME

I AM BACK IN MY OFFICE AT THE MUSEUM OF NATURAL History. We have had good news today. Ann Hanniball, our curator of collections, has found rabbit hair in a net made of Indian hemp. The net is over a thousand years old. It has been thought that Great Basin people carried nets such as this and engaged in "rabbit drives." In 1983, a technician corroborates the story. The connection stands.

Jay Nielsen, our artist, has completed a diorama of the brook trout. He just received notice that he won "judges choice" at the International Taxidermy Show. I saw his fish. They wear mythic robes.

And our director, Don Hague, has just returned from a special assignment in Taiwan, bringing back word that a trilobite and topaz from Utah now sit in the foyer of the National Museum of Natural Science there. They are metaphors for cultural exchange.

I am slowly coming to realize that all is not dead here: "past tense." But that remnants of life bear character. Horny Toad sits on a shelf with a sign saying, "Reptiles of Utah." I merely transport him back to Navajo sandstone with my imagination and see him making arrowheads for The People. I can find pieces of white shell here too.

A museum is not a replacement for the natural world, but a good place for urban pilgrims to visit. You can come here to collect your thoughts and remember animals you have seen or dreamed of. You can come here to learn the grace of sego lilies in the survival of a people. Old myths are dispelled. New myths are created.

I remember standing in front of a Fremont bracelet. It was a circle of prairie falcon talons laced together with rawhide. There was an aura I cannot explain. I wondered about the individual who had worn it, for what occasion it had been made. For a brief moment, I entered sacred time. Perhaps this is the performance of an artifact.

Mysteries surround me. I wear them as loose clothing. In the Anthropology Hall stands the Barrier Canyon mural, a reproduction of pictographs found in southeastern Utah. Huge figures rise staring out from the rock like ghosts. In time the flat surface takes on dimension. Four figures I thought to be in line form a square.

Sacred time. We cannot always live there. But if we know it exists, we can begin to experience the soul of the land. From here our stories will spill forth.

EPILOGUE

WE HAVE TRAVELED FAR TOGETHER. AND THERE IS MORE, much more. Story is a sacred visualization, a way of echoing experience. There are lessons along the way.

I have just returned once again from Navajoland. I am bruised and my friend has a fractured ankle. I am still sorting through what happened.

It was Monday. Having just arrived from Salt Lake City after ten hours on the road, we drove to the Chapter House and then to Red Mesa. Our pace was a little frenzied. The children were waiting for us. We all were primed. We were together for stories. The children knew it. We knew it. And there were others who knew—

Once at Red Mesa, we ran. It felt good to be out—out from driving, out from school, out with the rocks. We scattered across the slickrock like buckshot. Only our voices kept us together. We found water bordered by lizard tracks, where each child sank a handprint in wet clay. We found mosses, lichen, and cryptogams. We discovered tunnels of hardened sand, not yet mature enough to be rock. On hands and knees we entered the worlds of prairie dog and burrowing owl. Toward the end of the tunnel we found a nest resting on a precarious sandstone shingle— canyon wren's home. One by one we stood up outside the cavern. Agents of erosion. As our eyes adjusted to light, tumbleweeds blew this way and that.

We were explorers—unaware of the hazards associated with the country we were entering—the country of stories. Stories flew from one child to the next. My head was turning north, turning south, looking west and east. I couldn't catch them all. I couldn't focus on any one. Words were being lost. I became uncomfortable. Two of the children saw a horned lizard. They called him Grandfather. He darted under a rock. I missed him too.

Just then, I heard screams. To my right were shouts: "Rattlesnake!" To my left was Bruce Hucko, with his ankle crushed between boulders. With no time for fear, three of us ran to him and kneeled beside the rock. We pulled the slab toward us. It wouldn't move. We pushed the slab away from us. Still it wouldn't move. Not knowing what to do, I looked up. The rocks would not yield. The rattlesnake was on the other side of the arroyo. With his rattles shaking he looked like a gourd dancer. The next thing we knew, Bruce's foot was free.

Three hours later, Hucko was admitted to the San Juan

Hospital in Monticello, Utah, with a sheered tibia and fibula along with multiple fractures to the ankle.

Back at Red Mesa, forty-plus Navajo children and I were driving dirt roads in a scarlet, fifteen-passenger van. No wonder the Navajo call children "little people"—they are not children at all. They guided me with care and good humor over 250 miles of desert terrain. They told stories to each other, stories of skinwalkers with glowing eyes, of white owls, and the place where cracked stars blanket the bluff. With my hands gripping the steering wheel in ruts of soft sand, I was trembling inside. I watched the road. It started to rain.

Rattlesnake is the guardian of sacred things. We were in violation. In our enthusiasm to share we had forgotten the seriousness of context. A story is never random. It must be framed with fierce attention, trust, and affection. Telling a story is always an act of faith. Whenever order is broken, chaos is unleashed. Story is a sacred visualization. There are lessons along the way.

ACKNOWLEDGMENTS

ON THIS JOURNEY TO NAVAJOLAND, I HAVE HAD MANY GUIDES to whom I am indebted.

Dr. Florence Krall, chairman of Educational Studies at the University of Utah has been a powerful influence on how I have traveled. She is a visionary in curriculum for social change. She has been my mentor. Because of her, I see things differently.

Bruce Hucko, artist-in-residence at Montezuma Creek Elementary School, opened doors for the children and me. He gave us the time to be ourselves and taught me there are more commonalities than differences between non-Indian and Indian peoples. His energy is a dance upon the desert.

To the families and children of Red and White Mesa, El Paso and Phillips camp on the Utah Navajo Reservation I am especially grateful. Their graciousness and willingness to share formed the heart of this manuscript.

There have been other guides along the way who have opened my eyes to story and landscape: Barry Lopez, Simon Ortiz, Scott Momaday, Meg Brady, Ed Lueders, Peter Nabokov, Dolores LaChappelle, Bill Pinar, Ted Major, Katherine Nelson, and Donna House.

Others whose influence shaped the manuscript: Diane and John Tempest, Kathryn and Jack Tempest, Lettie and Sanky Dixon, Susan Parry, Fred Edwards, Lee and Ed Riddell, Lyn and Jan Dalebout, Olivette Trotter, Donna Land Maldonado, Beverly Crum, Kim Stark, John Schow, Janet Durham Winters, Carol Blackwell, Robert Mayer and Lynne Ann Tempest.

My colleagues at the Utah Museum of Natural History are family and I acknowledge their remarkable patience and flexibility with me as I was dreaming of turquoise skies and sage: Donald V. Hague, Director; Mary Gesicki, Curator of Education; Ann Hanniball, Curator of Collections; Frank De-Courten, Adjunct Curator of Geology; and Fran Minton, who trusted me from the beginning. To the entire staff, I am grateful.

Clifford Brycelea is a wonderful storyteller. Through his artistic perceptions he gives the Navajo stories form. I have appreciated his honesty and commitment to the ideas we have been working with. We have shared much. Thanks to Jackson Clark, Jr., and the Clark family at the Toh-Atin Gallery in Durango, Colorado, for introducing us.

I especially want to acknowledge Laurie Schieffelin, my editor at Scribners. Her sensitivity to language is inspiring. To her, I am indebted.

And to Brooke, who lives with the underside of all my stories.

NOTES

Prologue

Page 4, lines 14–25:
LUTHER, STANDING BEAR, *Land of the Spotted Eagle* (Boston, 1933), p. 26. Quoted in Peggy Beck and A. L. Walters, *The Sacred* (Tsaile, Ariz.: Navajo Community College, 1977), p. 60.

Page 4, lines 28–31:
RUTH UNDERHILL AND MARIA CHONA, "The Autobiography of a Papago Woman," *Memoirs of the American Anthropological Association*, No. 46 (Menasha, Wis.: 1936. Reprint. New York: Krause Reprint Co., 1974), p. 5.

Chapter 2

Page 23, lines 31, 32; page 24, lines 1–15:
GLADYS REICHARD, *Navaho Religion*, Bollingen Series (Princeton: Princeton University Press, 1950), pp. 21–22.

Chapter 3

Page 30, lines 24–30:
GLADYS REICHARD, *Navaho Religion*, Bollingen Series (Princeton: Princeton University Press, 1950), p. 14.

Page 31, lines 1–20:
ETHELOU YAZZIE, *Navajo History, Volume One* (Tsaile, Ariz.: Navajo Community College Press, 1971), p. 21.

Page 31, lines 27–29:
PEGGY BECK AND A. L. WALTERS, *The Sacred* (Tsaile, Ariz.: Navajo Community College Press, 1977), p. 90.

Page 31, lines 31, 32; page 32, lines 1–3:
FRANC NEWCOMB, *Navajo Folktales* (Santa Fe: Museum of Navajo Ceremonial Art, 1967), p. 88.

Page 32, lines 17, 18:
BECK AND WALTERS, *Op. cit.*, p. 95.

Page 33, lines 1–4:
YAZZIE, *Op. cit.*, p. 21.

Page 33, lines 9–12:
REICHARD, *Op. cit.*, p. 21.

Page 33, lines 13–18:
YAZZIE, *Op. cit.*, p. 17.

Page 33, lines 22–30:
KARL W. LUCKERT, *Navajo Mountain and Rainbow Bridge Religion* (Flagstaff, Ariz.: Museum of Northern Arizona, 1977), p. 51.

Page 33, line 31; page 34, lines 1–4:
Ibid., p. 50.

Page 34, lines 9–16:
LELAND C. WYMAN, *Sacred Mountains of the Navajo* (Flagstaff, Ariz.: Museum of Northern Arizona, 1967), p. 23.

Page 34, lines 20–26:
Ibid.

Page 35, lines 1–9:
Ibid., p. 24.

Page 35, lines 13–19:
Ibid.

Chapter 4

Page 40, line 19:
For the sake of my informant's privacy, I have chosen to change her name and use a traditional version of the birth of Changing Woman, already published, rather than violate her story which was told in confidence. Variations in origin myths are as common as the oral tradition itself, and inevitably responsible for personal alterations and interpretations.

Page 40, lines 20–33; page 41, lines 1–17:
GLADYS REICHARD, *Navaho Religion*, Bollingen Series (Princeton: Princeton University Press, 1950), pp. 408–409.
Page 42, lines 12–17:
Ibid., p. 410.
Page 42, lines 19–29; page 43, lines 1–5:
WASHINGTON MATTHEWS, *Navaho Legends* (Boston, New York: Houghton Mifflin Co., 1897; Reprint. New York: Kraus Reprint Co., 1976), p. 105.
Page 43, lines 27–29:
Ibid., p. 34.
Page 43, lines 1–2; page 44, lines 1, 2:
GARY WITHERSPOON, *Language and Art in the Navajo Universe* (Ann Arbor: University of Michigan Press, 1977), p. 23.
Page 44, lines 9–18:
P. E. GODDARD, "Navajo Texts," *Anthropological Papers of the American Museum of Natural History* 34 (1933): 175.

Chapter 5

Page 50, lines 8–17:
GLADYS REICHARD, *Navaho Religion*, Bollingen Series (Princeton: Princeton University Press, 1950), p. 487.
Page 53, lines 19–33; page 54, lines 1–7:
CHARLOTTE JOHNSON FRISBIE, *Kinaaldá* (Middletown, Conn.: Wesleyan University Press, 1967), p. 12.
Page 55, lines 4–9:
Ibid., p. 267.

Page 58, lines 16–28:
EDWARD S. AYENSU, "A Worldwide Role for the Healing Powers of Plants," *Smithsonian* (November, 1981): 92.

Chapter 6

Page 63, lines 19–32; page 64, lines 1–34; page 65, lines 1–13:
WASHINGTON MATTHEWS, *Navaho Legends* (Boston, New York: Houghton Mifflin Co., 1897. Reprint. New York: Kraus Reprint Co., 1976), pp. 120–121.

Page 66, lines 2–3:
GLADYS REICHARD, "Navajo Classification of Natural Objects," *Plateau* 28, no. 1 (1948): 7.

Page 66, lines 29–32; page 67, lines 1–3:
BARRY HOLSTUN LOPEZ, ed., "The American Indian Mind," *Quest* (September–October 1978): 123.

Page 67, lines 7–12:
FRANC JOHNSON NEWCOMB, *Navajo Omens and Taboos* (Sante Fe: The Rydal Press, 1940), F-5.

Page 68, lines 14–24:
Ibid.

Page 69, lines 28–29; page 70, lines 1–27:
Ibid.

Page 69, lines 5–9:
GARY WITHERSPOON, *Language and Art in the Navajo Universe* (Ann Arbor: University of Michigan Press, 1977), p. 13.

Page 69, lines 10–23:
Ibid., p. 18.

Page 69, lines 27–31; page 70, lines 1–7:
DONALD SANDER, *Navaho Symbols of Healing* (New York: Harcourt Brace Jovanovich, 1979), p. 13.

Page 70, lines 9–20:
CLYDE KLUCKHOLN AND DORTHEA LEIGHTON, *The Navaho* (New York: American Museum of Natural History, 1962), p. 308.

Page 70, lines 24–26:
WITHERSPOON, *Op. cit.*, p. 180.

Chapter 7

Page 78, lines 18–21:
WASHINGTON MATTHEWS, *Navaho Legends* (Boston, New York: Houghton Mifflin Co., 1897. Reprint. New York: Kraus Reprint Co., 1976), p. 71.
Page 79, lines 12–15:
W. W. HILL AND DOROTHY W. HILL, "Navaho Coyote Tales and Their Position in the Southern Athabaskan Group," *Journal of American Folklore* 58 (1945): p. 317.
Page 79, lines 20–32; page 80, lines 1–25:
Ibid., p. 328.
Page 82, lines 4–14:
MATTHEWS, *Op. cit.*, p. 77.
Page 84, lines 11–16:
W. W. HILL, *Navaho Warfare*, Yale University Publications in Anthropology, Number 5, 1936, p. 14.

Chapter 8

Page 91, lines 14, 15:
The traditional story of Changing-bear-maiden can be read in Washington Matthews's *Navaho Legends* (Boston, New York: Houghton Mifflin Co., 1897. Reprint. New York: Kraus Reprint Co., 1976), p. 103.

Additional notes on the bear in Navajo cosmology can be found in Gladys Reichard's *Navaho Religion*, Bollingen Series (Princeton: Princeton University Press, 1950), pp. 384–386.

Page 91, lines 27, 28:
Quote found on the back of a student's notebook at Navajo Community College in Tsaile, Ariz.

Page 92, lines 9–11:
KARL LUCKERT, *Navajo Hunter Tradition* (Tucson: University of Arizona Press, 1975), p. 40.
Page 93, lines 4, 5:
MATTHEWS, *Op. cit.*, p. 71.

Page 93, lines 20–22:
ETHELOU YAZZIE, *Navajo History, Volume I* (Tsaile, Ariz.:
Navajo Community College Press, 1971), p. 30.

Page 93, line 18:
In the Navajo origin myth, of which there are different versions, the "separation of the sexes" is an important element.
First Man decided to separate the men from the women. He
built a raft which carried the men to the other side of the river.
He wanted to prove that the women could not get along without them. Four men were left behind: Yellow Fox, Blue Fox,
Badger, and Coyote. These lustful characters soon became ex-
hausted from trying to meet the sexual demands of so many
women. Their desires, which seem unquenchable in the beginning, quickly disappeared. By and by, the sexes were re-
united, after both realized it would be terrible without each
other.

Page 94, lines 6, 7:
LUCKERT, *Op. cit.*, p. 33.
Page 94, lines 11, 12:
Ibid., p. 27.
Page 94, lines 12–20:
REICHARD, *Op. cit.*, p. 416.
Page 95, lines 17–19:
MATTHEWS, *Op. cit.*, p. 118.
Page 95, lines 23–25:
BARRE TOELKEN, "Prairie Dogs Cry For Rain," *Quest* (Septem-
ber–October, 1978): 115. ("The American Indian Mind," edi-
ted by Barry Lopez).

This allusion refers to Barre Toelken's story about the Navajo
belief relating rain to burrowing animals. In 1950, government
agents proposed to get rid of prairie dogs on some parts of the
reservation in order to protect the roots of the sparse desert
grass and thereby maintain some marginal grazing for sheep.
The Navajo objected, insisting, "If you kill off all the prairie
dogs, there will be no one to cry for the rain." The amused

government officials assured the Navajo there was no correlation between rain and prairie dogs and carried out their experiment. The outcome was surprising only to the government. Today the area near Chilchinbito, Arizona, has become virtually a wasteland with very little grass. Without the ground-turning process of the burrowing animals, the soil has become solidly packed, unable to accept rain. The result: fierce runoff whenever it rains. What sparse vegetation was once there has been carried off by flooding waters.

Page 96, line 10:
LUCKERT, *Op. cit.*, p. 21.

Begochidi and Black-god were those among the creators of the game animals. They put down six buffalo skins on top of each other: white, blue, yellow, and shiny buffalo skins. Then on these they poured juices of turquoise, the saps of growing plants and their pollen, the essence of white shell, puddles of water, running rivulets, and all the plants. Over these they put as cover again six buffalo skins on top of each other. Then the gods started singing. Inside it began to move.

Chapter 9

Page 100, line 15:
OSWALD WERNER, "A Taxonomic View of the Traditional Navajo Universe" (Evanston, Ill.: Northwestern University), 21, 22.
Page 100, lines 19–23:
BARRY HOLSTUN LOPEZ, *Of Wolves and Men* (New York: Charles Scribner's Sons, 1978), p. 102.
Page 100, lines 25–33:
BARRY HOLSTUN LOPEZ, ed., "The American Indian Mind." *Quest* (September–October 1978), p. 102.
Ibid., p. 122.
Page 101, lines 1–3:
GREGORY BATESON, *Mind And Nature* (New York: E. P. Dutton, 1979), p. 5.

Page 101, line 5:
KARL W. LUCKERT, *The Navajo Hunting Tradition* (Tuscon: University of Arizona Press, 1975), pp. 29–31.
Page 101, line 5:
Ibid., p. 31.
Page 101, line 5:
Ibid., p. 38.
Page 105, lines 1–9:
Ibid.
Page 105, lines 29–32; page 106, lines 1–13:
N. SCOTT MOMADAY, "Native American Attitudes to the Environment," *Seeing with a Native Eye.* Edited by Walter Holden Capps. (New York: Harper & Row, 1976), p. 82.
Page 110, lines 1–6:
Ibid., p. 83.

Chapter 10

Page 110, lines 1–6:
BARRE TOELKEN, "Seeing with a Native Eye: How Many Sheep Will It Hold?" *Seeing with a Native Eye* (New York: Harper & Row, 1976), p. 12.
Page 110, lines 11–22:
GLADYS REICHARD, *Spider Woman* (Santa Fe, New Mexico: Rio Grande Press, 1934), frontispiece.
Page 110, lines 26, 27; page 111, lines 1–8:
CLYDE KLUCKHOLN AND DORTHEA LEIGHTON, *The Navaho* (Cambridge, Mass.: Harvard University Press, 1946), p. 39.
Page 111, lines 24–31; page 112, lines 1–22:
REICHARD, *Op. cit.*, p. 122.
Page 112, lines 26–29:
KLUCKHOHN, *Op. cit.* p. 70.
Page 113, line 3:
SEE INSERT FOR FOOTNOTE 6.
Page 113, lines 11–16:
CLYDE BENALLY, *Dinéji Nákéé' Nááhané: A Utah Navajo History* (San Juan School District, Monticello, Utah: University of Utah Printing Services, 1982), p. 159.

For a more in-depth account of the sheep reduction program and decisions made by Charles H. Burke and John Collier, commissioners of Indian Affairs during this period, see Benally, pp. 159–164.

Chapter 12

Page 133, line 23:
It is believed by the Navajo that the San Juan River is male and the Colorado River is female, the former being swift, the later more gentle in its flow. I have heard from others that where the San Juan and the Colorado Rivers once joined (now covered by Lake Powell) the San Juan mounted the Colorado, as the male waters flowed over the female waters. It was at this marriage of rivers that many "water children" were born.

Page 135, lines 1–3:
LAURENS VAN DER POST, *A Story Like the Wind* (New York: Harcourt Brace Jovanovich, 1972), frontispiece.

Page 135, lines 13, 14:
Letter received from Simon Ortiz, May 25, 1980.

Page 135, lines 14–16:
Conversations with Simon Ortiz, Albuquerque, New Mexico, May 23–27, 1980.

Page 135, lines 17–19:
BARRY HOLSTUN LOPEZ, "Interior and Exterior Landscapes." Lecture given in Jackson Hole, Wyoming, at the Teton Science School on April 10, 1981.

Page 135, lines 20–22:
ALDO LEOPOLD, *A Sand County Almanac* (New York: Oxford University Press, 1949. Reprint. New York: Ballantine Books, 1970), p. 264.

Page 135, lines 26–29:
GREGORY BATESON, *Mind and Nature* (New York: E. P. Dutton, 1979), p. 13.

Page 135, lines 30–33; page 136, lines 1–5:
Conversation with Herb Blatchford, Albuquerque, New Mexico, May 26, 1980.

Page 136, line 8:
Ortiz, conversations cited.

Chapter 13

Page 142, line 16:
The sego lily, *Calochortus nuttallii*, is credited with saving the lives of many Mormon settlers, especially during the fall of 1848 when crops were damaged by a horde of crickets. The thick scaled bulb is a delicacy, tasting much like a raw potato. In gratitude, the sego lily was named Utah's state flower.

Page 142, line 23:
Conversation with Barre Toelken, Fife Folklore Conference, Logan, Utah, June 10, 1983.

BIBLIOGRAPHY

Astov, Margot. "The Concept of Motion as the Psychological Leitmotif of Navaho Life and Literature." *Journal of American Folklore* 64 (1950).

Bateson, Gregory. *Mind and Nature.* New York: E. P. Dutton, 1979.

Beck, Peggy V. and Walters, A. L. *The Sacred.* Tsaile, Ariz.: Navajo Community College, 1977.

Benally, Clyde. *Diné Ii Nákéé' Nááhane, A Utah Navajo History.* San Juan School District, Monticello, Utah: University of Utah Printing Services, 1982.

Britt, Claude. "Early Navajo Astronomical Pictographs." In *Archaeo-Astronomy in Pre-Columbian America,* edited by Anthony F. Aveni. Austin: University of Texas Press, 1975.

CAPP, WALTER HOLDEN, ED. *Seeing with a Native Eye*. New York: Harper & Row, 1976.

CIRLOT, J. E. *Dictionary of Symbols*. New York: Philosophical Library, 1962.

ELMORE, FRANCIS H. *Ethnobotany of the Navajo*. Albuquerque: University of New Mexico Press, 1943.

FRISBIE, CHARLOTTE JOHNSON. *Kinaaldá*. Middletown, Conn.: Wesleyan University Press, 1967.

HAILE, FATHER BERARD. *Beautyway: A Navaho Ceremonial*. Bollingen Series. New York: Pantheon Books, 1957.

————. "Navaho Chantways and Ceremonials," *American Anthropologist* 40 (1938): 639–52.

————. *Soul Concepts of the Navaho*. St. Michael's, Arizona: St. Michael's Press. Reprint, 1975.

————. *Starlore Among the Navaho*. Sante Fe, New Mexico: Museum of Navajo Ceremonial Art, 1947.

HARDING, ESTHER. *Woman's Mysteries*. New York: G. P. Putnam's Sons for C. G. Jung Foundation, 1971.

HILL, W. W. AND HILL, DOROTHY W. "Navaho Coyote Tales and Their Position in the Southern Athabaskan Group," *Journal of American Folklore* 58 (1945): 317–43.

JENNING, JESS D. *Prehistory of Utah and the Eastern Great Basin*, Anthropological Papers, No. 98, Salt Lake City: University of Utah, 1978.

JOHNSON, CHRISTIE. *Southwest Mammals: Navajo Beliefs & Legends*. San Juan School District, Monticello, Utah: University of Utah Printing Services, 1979.

KLUCKHOHN, CLYDE AND LEIGHTON, DORTHEA. *The Navaho*. Cambridge, Mass.: Harvard University Press, 1946.

LEOPOLD, ALDO. *Sand County Almanac*. New York: Oxford University Press, Inc., 1949. Reprint. New York: Ballantine Books, 1970.

LINK, MARGARET SCHEVIL. *The Pollen Path*. Stanford: Stanford University Press, 1956.

LOPEZ, BARRY HOLSTUN. "The American Indian Mind." *Quest*, September–October, 1978.

————. *Of Wolves and Men*. New York: Charles Scribner's Sons, 1978.

LUCKERT, KARL W. *The Navajo Hunting Tradition.* Tucson: University of Arizona Press, 1975.

————. *Navajo Mountain and Rainbow Bridge Religion.* Flagstaff, Ariz.: Museum of Northern Arizona, 1977.

MATTHEWS, WASHINGTON. "Navajo Names for Plants." *American Naturalist* 20 (1886): 767–77.

————. *Navaho Legends.* Boston, New York: Houghton Mifflin Co., 1897. Reprint. New York: Kraus Reprint Co., 1976.

McNELEY, JAMES KALE. *Holy Wind in Navajo Philosophy.* Tucson: University of Arizona Press, 1981.

NEWCOMB, FRANC JOHNSON. *Navajo Bird Tales.* Wheaton: The Theosophical Publishing House, 1970.

PARSONS, ELSIE CLEWS. "Navaho Folktales." *Journal of American Folklore* 36, (1923): 368–75.

RADIN, PAUL. *The Trickster.* New York: Schocken Books, 1956.

REICHARD, GLADYS. "Navajo Classification of Natural Objects." *Plateau,* Volume 21, no. 1, 1948.

————. *Navaho Religion.* Bollingen Series. Princeton: Princeton University Press, 1950.

————. *Spider Woman.* Glorieta, New Mexico: Rio Grande Press, Inc., 1934.

SAAD ANĄ́ĄH SINIL; *Dual Language.* Edited by Martha A. Austin. Chinle, Ariz.: Navajo Curriculum Center, 1972.

SANDNER, DONALD. *Navaho Symbols of Healing.* New York: Harcourt Brace Jovanovich, 1979.

SPENCER, KATHERINE. "Reflections of Social Life in the Navaho Origin Myth." University of New Mexico Publications in Anthropology 3 (1947).

TOZZER, ALFRED M. "A Note on Star-lore among the Navajos." *Journal of American Folklore* 21 (1908): 28–32.

VAN VALKENBURGER, RICHARD F. *Navajo Sacred Places.* New York: Garland Publishers Inc., 1974.

WATSON, EDITH L. *Navajo Sacred Places.* Window Rock: Navajoland Publications, 1964.

WERNER, OSWALD, "A Taxonomic View of the Traditional Navajo Universe." Evanston, Ill.: Northwestern University.

WHEELRIGHT, MARY C. *Navajo Creation Myth.* Sante Fe: Museum of Navajo Ceremonial Art, 1942.

WITHERSPOON, GARY. *Language and Art in the Navajo Universe.* Ann Arbor: University of Michigan Press, 1977.

————. "A New Look at Navajo Social Organization" *American Anthropologist,* No. 72, 1970.

WYMAN, LELAND C. *Sacred Mountains of the Navajo.* Flagstaff, Ariz.: Museum of Northern Arizona, 1967.

WYMAN, LELAND C. AND BAILEY, FLORA L. "Navaho Indian Ethno-Entomology." *University of N. M. Publications in Anthropology,* No. 12, 1964.

WYMAN, LELAND C. AND HARRIS, STUART K. "The Ethnobotany of the Kayenta Navaho." *University of N. M. Publications in Biology,* No. 5, 1951.

————. "Navaho Indian Medical Ethnobotany." *University of New Mexico Bulletin* 366, 1941.

YAZZIE, ETHELOU. *Navajo History, Volume I.* Tsaile, Ariz.: Navajo Community College Press, 1971.